AUTHOR:
Jack Harrison
info@mortonsbooks.co.uk

PAGE DESIGN:
Craig Lamb
design_lamb@btinternet.com

COVER DESIGN:
Justin Blackamore

COVER ARTWORK:
John Fox
www.design-phoenix.com

PRODUCTION EDITOR:
Dan Sharp

REPROGRAPHICS:
Paul Fincham
Jonathan Schofield

ADVERTISING:
Sue Keily
skeily@mortons.co.uk

MARKETING MANAGER:
Charlotte Park

COMMERCIAL DIRECTOR:
Nigel Hole

PUBLISHING DIRECTOR:
Dan Savage

PUBLISHER:
Steve O'Hara

Images marked ✪ are in the public
domain. Images marked ✱ are
published under a Creative Commons
License, creativecommons.org

PRINTED BY:
William Gibbons and Sons,
Wolverhampton

ISBN:
978-1-911276-97-5

PUBLISHED BY:
Mortons Media Group Ltd,
Media Centre,
Morton Way,
Horncastle,
Lincolnshire
LN9 6JR

COPYRIGHT:
Mortons Media Group Ltd
2022 all rights reserved.

CONT

G000277844

008 CHAPTER 1
The Pacific Theatre

010 CHAPTER 2
On the road to war

018 CHAPTER 3
The day of infamy

040 CHAPTER 4
The Southern
Resource Area

046 CHAPTER 5
Critical Japanese
mistakes

052 CHAPTER 6
Reaction and
retribution

062 CHAPTER 7
America's fight back

064 CHAPTER 8
America cracks
the code

066 CHAPTER 9
The battle lines
are drawn

070 CHAPTER 10
From Coral Sea
to Midway:
America
turns the tide

108 CHAPTER 11
The Pacific War
after Midway

114 CHAPTER 12
A symbolic battle
in the skies

122 CHAPTER 13
Submarine warfare

124 CHAPTER 14
Allied offensives

128 CHAPTER 15
Resistance and
surrender

Acknowledgements

The one-line mentions above do not do enough
justice to those who have used their
considerable skills and talents to help produce
this 132-page edition that you see before you.
Starting, quite literally, from the front,
I cannot speak highly enough about the
superb work of cover artist John Fox
(www.design-phoenix.com). In all the
research I have undertaken for this volume,
I have seen few better artistic depictions
of the Battle of Midway. He has truly managed
to bring the past to life.

I must also thank the efforts of designers
Craig Lamb (pages) and Justin Blackamore
(cover), as well as production editor Dan

Sharp who have all been instrumental in
bringing my chosen words and images together.
As have Paul Fincham and Jonathan Schofield;
working with 80-year-old photography is a
challenging task for even the most skilled
picture desk, and they have certainly done the
incredible range of material available the justice
it deserves. And it would also be remiss of me to
not mention the friends, family and loved ones
who have encouraged and supported the
research and writing involved in this project.
It's been a great privilege to present this
fascinating story, but it's certainly not a one-
person job. My thanks to everyone who has
played a part.

Flagship *Akagi* under attack

Artwork: John Fox

An extended view of our cover artwork depicting the moments just before Japanese carrier *Akagi* suffered a fatal hit during action on June 4, 1942, at the Battle of Midway. The background aircraft is the Douglas SBD-3 Dauntless of junior grade Lieutenant John Kroeger – his 1000lb bomb just missing. In the foreground is the Dauntless of VB6 squadron leader Lieutenant Commander Richard Halsey Best whose strike penetrated *Akagi's* deck and caused the damage that would sink her the following day.

Pacific War

The Battle of Midway. Most have heard of it, many know it as a turning point of the Pacific War. But how did this major engagement, pitting the inexperienced US Navy against the battle-hardened Japanese sea forces, come to be such a significant chapter in the histories of both nations? It is my aim to shed some light on the answer in the 132 pages of this volume.

After the Pacific War burst explosively into being on December 7, 1941, Japan enjoyed near-total domination in the vast Theatre for a clear six months – and it was no fluke. Japan had emerged from the Great War of 1914-1918 as one of the few 'winners', having used the conflict to enhance its own aims of Asian dominance by taking control of territory from Germany. It had now positioned itself as the key power in the Asia-Pacific region, and both Europe and America would need to take notice.

While the complex web of treaties that followed the war were intended to prevent further violence and quell global militarism, they floundered in the face of worldwide economic turmoil, resource shortages, and other crises such as the devastating Spanish flu pandemic. And although much of Europe and the US were keen to embark on a period of peace, Japan remained far more open to the financial and territorial benefits that war could bring. It was this combination that allowed for a deep-rooted nationalist movement to arise in the country, and as the rest of the world tried to avoid further bloodshed, Japan looked increasingly to its new and powerful Imperial Navy to exert its will across the region and expand its new mini Empire into something far larger.

When the 353 fighters and bombers of the Combined Fleet began attacking the US Navy at Pearl Harbor on what was aptly termed a 'day of infamy' it was described as a surprise attack; yet perhaps it shouldn't have been. A Japanese advance had been brewing for more than a decade, and the raid was part of a carefully orchestrated series of operations that established Japan as the premier player in the Asia-Pacific region. Its expansion was well prepared and almost perfectly executed, and on the surface Japan appeared unbeatable.

As its Imperial Navy finalised arrangements to secure the final pieces of the Pacific puzzle, few in Japan could have predicted what was to come next as a resurgent and vengeful America hit back. Through a combination of brilliance, resilience and good fortune, the US managed to outmanoeuvre its enemy to win a tentative tactical victory at the Battle of the Coral Sea in May 1942. A month later in early June, it then showed the first signs of the terrible power it could wield by destroying four of Japan's prized aircraft carriers, a blow from which the enemy would never recover.

Soon after, America and its Allied partners launched a string of successful, albeit violent, offensives from the south that pushed Japan slowly but surely out of its Pacific strongholds and culminated in its eventual defeat. It was a remarkable turnaround.

How had it happened? There's no one single answer. Japan had certainly misread how America would react to an attack on its forces at Pearl Harbor, for all its superiority it soon emerged that there were holes in Japanese strategical thinking, America was able to turn its vast industrial potential to a war effort, and US code breakers managed to give their forces a crucial advantage against a more powerful enemy.

The way in which these various circumstances came together to shift momentum in favour of America is, in my own humble opinion, where the Pacific War was won and lost – and it is this story that is told here. I sincerely hope that you find it as interesting and informative to read as I have found it to research and write.

Jack Harrison
Author

◆

Pacific War, released to mark the 80th anniversary of the Battle of Midway, is intended as a follow-up edition to *Pearl Harbor: 80th Anniversary*. Released in September 2021, my first publication in this series focused on the events of December 7, 1941, and studied their impact in America, Japan and the wider world. This publication picks up the story to examine Japan's early dominance in the wake of its devastating victory in Hawaii, before attempting to uncover how America defied the odds to launch a fightback that would culminate in unconditional Japanese surrender.

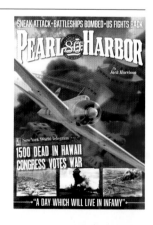

CHAPTER 1

Soldiers of Japan's Imperial Army are pictured in Korea during the conflict with Russia. The country's forces were now a match for any major world power. ○

The Pacific Theatre

W hile the world's attention was fixated on events in Europe during the 1920s and 1930s, a fierce and increasingly bitter rivalry was growing between the United States and Japan as each tried to dominate the Pacific region.

The European situation was primarily political – the aftermath of the First World War providing ideal conditions for the growth of aggressive extremist views – but the situation in the Pacific had more to do with economics. Conflicting US and Japanese interests centred on their mutually exclusive desire to control and exploit the region's abundant natural resources rather than ideological differences.

When hostilities between the two nations did eventually break out, the ensuing clash would rank among the most catastrophic and brutal in history. It was the outcome of a decades-long deterioration of relations; the resulting devastation a reflection of the extended period during which America and Japan had postured and provoked one another.

It is almost impossible to pinpoint an exact date when relations between the two countries began to sour. Certainly there were clear warning signs – such as Japanese aggression in China in the early 1930s – but the rivalry had been established much earlier and was more rooted in what the two nations had in common.

They had each undergone a dramatic transformation from insular and awkward to modern, industrialised, nationalistic and militaristic.

Before the 1900s, there appeared to be little threat of a breakdown of relations across the Pacific Ocean, but the respective actions of the US and Japan during that time sowed the seeds for the grand battle which was to come...

The foundations for future conflict

Both of them could be regarded as 'new' countries looking to establish themselves. Neither was lacking in history – America had seen European colonists displacing the pre-existing native population and Japan had traditions stretching back centuries – but neither had really existed as a unified nation strong enough to make its presence felt on the world stage.

For both countries, this changed in the early to middle part of the 19th century as technological advances brought about an industrial revolution. The invention of new machines brought about sweeping changes – agriculture required fewer workers and the people who were displaced went to work in city-based factories instead. As the cities grew, the process of sweeping away the old established order began.

This economic and societal change was precipitated politically in America by its declaration of independence from Great Britain in 1776 and the subsequent victory of American forces in the revolutionary war, two events that gave birth to a new entity – the United States of America. The situation was mirrored in Japan by the Meiji Restoration; the instigators of this movement fearful of the country's

vulnerability to aggressive actions by European powers and intent on seeing Japan catch up. It was from the beginning of this period in 1868 that the Empire of Japan arose.

The leaders of the two reborn societies put in place governmental systems and social structures that differed dramatically from one another, but essentially each had the same core purpose – to assume complete control of its own destiny and ensure that it would never have to bow to European demands.

With the rapid growth of manufacturing industry in the two nations came the need for raw materials and new markets in which to sell the resulting products. Both countries began to lay the groundwork for their own 'economic empires'. They were initially less concerned with the acquisition of land, than with securing unfettered access to lucrative trade deals that were up for grabs in Asia, Australia and throughout the Pacific.

In America, the descendants of the original European settlers spread out across the continent, eventually reaching the Pacific coastline in numbers. The natural barrier of the water would not stop the expansion, however, and before long the US would set its sights on exerting influence beyond its borders. To those in power it seemed as if the best way to prevent any entanglement in European affairs was for America to claim it's own 'sphere of influence' which, it was decided, included all of the Americas.

It might have been a near century-long process, but the appetite for advancement and economic growth was too great for the US to stop there and following a brief military engagement with Spain in 1898 it now found itself in possession of territories in the Caribbean – and more significantly out to the west in the Pacific. This move brought America face-to-face with the Empire of Japan, itself intent on establishing its own area of influence in the areas immediately surrounding its natural borders, and also pursuing a strategy of economic freedom and prosperity.

At the turn of the century, US and Japanese interests were actually aligned and there were many instances of co-operation between the pair. Both countries supported the idea of an 'open door' policy toward China that would allow access to its resource-rich regions for trading and potential investment, and as a result US president Theodore Roosevelt acted as peacemaker in the negotiations which spawned The Treaty of Portsmouth – an agreement between Russia and Japan that

A Japanese print shows the country's successful assault on Port Arthur. The battle was one of the first major demonstrations of Japan's new naval strength. ✪

formally ended war between the two in 1905. Japan's apparent commitment to equal opportunity with regard to trade in China meant American public and political opinion swayed in favour of Japan.

The brokering of the treaty proved to be the final significant act of US-Japanese co-operation before the outbreak of war in the Pacific, however, and subsequent years would see an ever-growing series of disagreements and confrontations centred around their respective interests in the territories of the Pacific and trade access to Southeast Asia.

The Treaty of Portsmouth

One of the western nations that Japan challenged in its efforts to establish itself as a world power was Russia. By 1904 the two had gone through several years of disputes over control of Manchuria – a region of China with great economic potential and an area that would prove to be a pivotal zone in the Pacific Theatre.

The Russians had entered Manchuria during the first Sino-Japanese War of 1894-1895 – a conflict between Japan and China's Qing Empire primarily concerning control over Korea – and it'd been joined by Germany and France as part of a 'triple intervention' that sought to limit Japan's ability to capitalise financially on its close proximity to the territory, forcing it to give up control of ports there.

One of those was Port Arthur, a warm-water facility with huge commercial and strategic attributes. Committed to breaking free from the yoke of European control, Japan attacked the Russian fleet stationed there in 1904 in a surprise attack and forced an early victory. Throughout the next year the two countries' armed forces clashed repeatedly and while it was Japan that managed to rack up most victories, they came at an unprecedented cost with casualties on both sides in the tens of thousands and the severe loss of military equipment, including prized ships.

Short it may have been, but the war had two significant outcomes. The first was the dramatic revelation to the world that the Japanese Empire – a country that just a half-

century before had been relatively obscure and unengaged with global events – had become a powerful military outfit with tremendous capabilities and resources. Second, as with America's war with Spain, it showed that Japan would go to whatever lengths necessary to protect its economic interests overseas; in fact, considering the losses it suffered, it demonstrated that it was willing to go far further than the US in this regard.

Those losses, however, did eventually begin to tell on Japan – and it became apparent that the strain of war was greater than any potential victory it could achieve. The situation was likewise in Russia, and in 1905 both countries sought a negotiated end to the violence. Japan invited President Roosevelt to oversee proceedings, and he welcomed representatives of both nations to Portsmouth, New Hampshire later in the year to begin peace talks.

Roosevelt had actually been buoyed by Japan's military success – the emphatic statement that the time of European domination was well and truly at an end being something he and all Americans could support. He was, however, cautious of Manchuria falling into total Japanese control and so – with his own interests in mind – aimed to conclude a deal that maintained a balance of power and equal opportunity for trade not just for Russia and Japan, but America also.

Jurisdiction over the ports of Manchuria was a central component of the talks, as were potential reparations and future ownership of

A postcard issued shortly after the deal was agreed shows the main signatories of the Treaty of Portsmouth. ✪

Sakhalin Island – a large territory off Japan's northern coast. Neither side budged initially, but both knew they lacked the resources and finances to sustain further hostilities so eventually came to a compromise that saw Russian influence curtailed in Manchuria and Korea, but retention of control over the northern part of Sakhalin Island and no requirement to pay an indemnity to the enemy. The agreement was ratified as the Treaty of Portsmouth.

Roosevelt won a Nobel peace prize for his role in the talks and, while they did succeed in establishing détente, Japan and Russia had reason to resent the outcome having not managed to achieve all of their respective aims. Attention in Russia would soon turn to the growing escalation of tension in Europe, but for Japan expansion in Manchuria, China and beyond into the Pacific became an ever-more tantalising proposition. It was a risky strategy, and it put the nation on a collision course with the United States.

CHAPTER 2

On the road to war

Rival economic and territorial ambitions laid the foundation for the Pacific War, and China would be the setting for the opening act of the epic and devastating drama about to ensue...

While Japan had to re-evaluate its tactics in the wake of its expensive conflict with Russia, its strategy of extending its influence across Asia remained unaltered. To further develop as an international power it became clear to Japanese leaders that the country needed a deeper economy and greater pool of resources to call upon.

The same thoughts were forming across the Pacific in America where Theodore Roosevelt's administration had significantly expanded US interests overseas in the name of cash and asset generation. The fact that the two had competing aims caused concern on both sides of the ocean, and the contrasting ways in which they went about achieving them would become the cornerstone of the tensions between the two that would eventually lead to war.

New century, new world powers

For the US, expansion was pursued by diplomatic means and through support for its burgeoning capitalist business sector. Maintaining its isolationist tendencies, central government refrained from direct involvement in international affairs – but did what it could to promote American business interests abroad, often wading into murky waters as it used various means and back-channels to manipulate foreign affairs.

Two notable examples of this were in Hawaii, where American government representatives had encouraged and even orchestrated elements of a coup d'état against the Hawaiian royal family that would eventually result in US annexation of the territory; and in Colombian-controlled Panama, where President Roosevelt – after his plans for a channel linking the Atlantic and Pacific were rejected by the Colombian senate – actively supported Panamanian rebels in their efforts to declare independence. Once this had been achieved, the US purchased control of the Panama Canal Zone for $10 million and Roosevelt's waterway was built.

It was a different story in Japan. While the American nation had been built on a complex political foundation that promoted its three branches of government – complete with checks and balances – more ancient traditions ran through the new Empire of Japan which gave a high level of control to its emperor and also placed an enormous amount of autocratic power within the different strands of its military.

While the US continued with its diplomacy – and its more subversive tactics – Japan was far more transparent and was not afraid to use military might to force through its aims. With the Treaty of Portsmouth having negated Russian influence in the area, in the early 20th century Japan pushed the boundaries of its agreements with America regarding free enterprise in China by consolidating its position in Manchuria.

Although tensions would boil over into other issues – institutional discrimination against Japanese-American immigrants on the west coast of the United States being one of the major examples – it was Manchuria, and wider problems in China, which proved to be a continuous sticking point. The outbreak of war in Europe in 1914 meant a temporary cessation of diplomatic

A *Holland 1*-class submarine, the first ever Japanese sub, that was purchased during the Russo-Japanese War. ✪

The rise of the Imperial Japanese Navy

In 1905 the Imperial Japanese Navy began building the battleship *Satsuma*, at the time the largest warship in the world. ✪

The Japanese seaplane carrier *Wakamiya* – it was from this ship that the world's first sea-launched air raids originated in 1914. ✪

Hosho, the world's first purpose-built aircraft carrier, completed in 1922. ✪

back-and-forth as both America and Japan sided with the Entente Powers against Germany – Japan providing military support in Asia. However, much to America's dismay, Japan used the war to extend its enterprises in China while the Imperial Japanese Navy – which had become a near-autonomous institution in Japan's political and military set-up – pushed out into the Pacific and wrestled various island groups from German hands.

By the end of the conflict there was no doubt that Japan had become one of the leading world powers, and played a key role in postwar negotiations and settlements as one of the brokers of the Versailles peace treaty and a founding member of the League of Nations. Japan's emergence wasn't necessarily viewed as an out-and-out threat in the US – but the increasing frequency of its endeavours in China and further afield caused alarm, as did the frightening capability of its navy, which was now one of the most advanced in the world and had been utilised to devastating effect against Russia in 1904 and Germany throughout 1914-1918. The failure of postwar treaties to quell fears of another European war and the ever-increasing scope and power of Japan's military over its foreign affairs approach were further areas of concern.

In response, US Secretary of State Charles Evans Hughes invited Japan and seven other nations to Washington in 1921 with two primary aims: striking an agreement on how each would pursue its policies in East Asia, and reaching an accord on naval disarmament and limitations. The meeting – and subsequent gatherings in 1922 – became known as the Washington Naval Conference.

There were three major treaties agreed at the conference, and although they would ultimately fall short of their goal to prevent tensions between Japan and America evolving into war, their implementation did manage to uphold and maintain a status quo in Asia and the Pacific for the best part of the next decade.

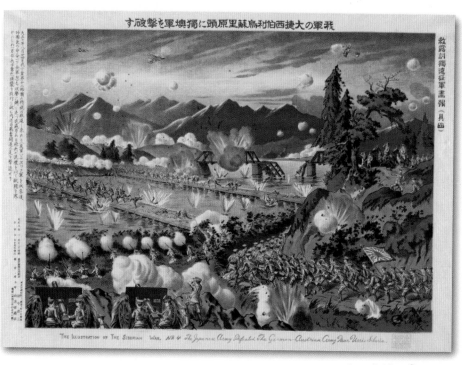

A Japanese lithograph that historians believe shows the Imperial Japanese Army fighting German troops in the German colony of Tsingtao during the First World War. The original caption locates the action as being in Siberia after 1918, but there's no evidence of German soldiers being in Asia during this time.

The Washington Naval Conference of 1921. ✪

Treaties of the Washington Naval Conference

The Five-Power Treaty
Signed by the US, Great Britain, Japan, France and Italy

This was the centrepiece agreement and called for the signatories to maintain a set ratio of warship tonnage – America and Britain allowed 500,000 tons, Japan 300,000 tons and France and Italy 175,000 tons; the numbers reflecting the fact that the US and UK had to maintain fleets in both the Atlantic and Pacific. The nations also had to scrap older vessels and they were prevented from building new capital ships. While the system was widely regarded as a success, the tonnage controls didn't cover certain classes and so prompted a new race to build cruisers. Aside from its hardware restrictions, the treaty also recognised American, British and Japanese bases in the Pacific but outlawed any expansion.

The Four-Power Treaty
Signed by the US, Great Britain, Japan and France

The countries agreed to consult with each other in the event of a future crisis in East Asia before taking unilateral action. The strength of Japan's military and its ability to act quickly in the region were key factors in this part of the agreement, as was the need to replace the 1902 Anglo-Japanese Treaty – American policymakers fearing that if war with Japan were to occur then Britain would be obligated to side with the Japanese. The treaty ensured that none of them were committed to involvement in any argument or confrontation between other members, but put in place a mechanism that would hopefully defuse any incident and prevent it from developing into full-scale military action.

The Nine-Power Treaty
Signed by the US, Great Britain, Japan, France, Italy, Belgium, the Netherlands, Portugal and China

The final agreement of the conferences formalised America's long-held 'open door' approach to China and guaranteed that all nations would have an equal chance to do business there. The treaty did recognise Japanese dominance of Manchuria, but also reaffirmed China's territorial integrity – a key element that was designed to end Japanese expansion. For its part, China agreed not to discriminate against any country seeking commercial opportunity. As would later become apparent, the one major flaw was that it called for further consultation in response to any violation and so lacked a method by which to enforce its rules.

Japanese forces disarm surrendering Chinese personnel following the occupation of Manchuria and the establishment of Manchuko. ✪

The interwar years

The Washington Naval Conference – along with the complex web of additional treaties and agreements designed to settle the issues which prompted the First World War and prevent a repeat – managed to uphold a relatively peaceful status across the globe in the 1920s, but trouble was brewing. Conflict had been costly – particularly for the losing sides – and many European economies went through periods of desperate struggle.

A soldier raises the Japanese Empire's flag above a captured Chinese army building in Mukden the day after it moved into the city. ✪

It was the same story in Japan where, despite its light industry having established its place in the world market as a result of the war, its economy went into recession in 1926. The circumstances were slightly different in the US – and the decline would come a little later – but it wasn't immune and even though it had enjoyed a relative boom in its economy in the early 1920s it meant many of its citizens had the opportunity to borrow; and they did so to invest in the stock market. It was a house of cards waiting to collapse, and it did on Tuesday, October 29, 1929 with the Wall Street Crash and the onset of the debilitating Great Depression.

It meant that the 1930s began with global economic turmoil, and it was an environment that sparked a wave of nationalism and militaristic tendencies across some of the world's super powers – most notably in Germany, Italy and Japan. The actions of Germany and Italy were of immediate threat to Europe, and the US – concentrating on its own financial recovery – held true to its principles that it would not entangle itself in affairs on the other side of the Atlantic. Westwards across the Pacific, however, America had a problem.

Japanese strength lay in its manufacturing prowess and industrial capability, but as a geographically small nation it lacked the huge quantity of raw materials it needed and so became dependent on western supplies. With political instability and economic pressure creating unrest in the country, a militarist faction – led by army general Hideki Tojo, a member of Japan's fascist party – was able to assume large swathes of power within the country's corridors of power. Tojo, and other military leaders under the direction of Emperor Hirohito, refocused attention on expansion in East Asia where the necessary resources were plentiful and far cheaper to come by. Pressure was building, and it resulted in an event that could be argued as being the first military engagement of the Pacific War – the Mukden Incident.

Manchuria had been a hotspot for international wrangling for many years, and on September 18, 1931, a small explosion occurred on a Japanese-owned railway line in the region. Damage was negligible – so much so that a passing train just minutes later was unimpeded – but the Imperial Japanese Army blamed Chinese nationalists for the 'attack' and used it as a pretext to invade. Untrained and ill-equipped Chinese forces could do little, and Japan achieved full occupation of Manchuria without difficulty or opposition. The identity of the 'attackers' remains controversial today – evidence suggesting that the act was carried out by Japanese military officers intent on provoking aggravation, looking for a reason to flex their muscles and wanting an excuse to take control of the region.

The freedom enjoyed by Japan's military branches certainly makes this theory a viable one, and it's supported by the fact that back in Tokyo there was shock at how far Japan's aggression had gone. With Army and Navy leaders holding constitutional power in Japan's government, however, they were able to force through their aims – which also had support from the people – and politicians were powerless to stop the invading forces from claiming victory after victory in the Chinese towns and cities along the 730-mile long stretch of railway.

Whether the Mukden Incident was an ill-advised act of aggression by Chinese nationalists or a carefully orchestrated plan by the Japanese military as a precursor for invasion, Japan's relentless march through Manchuria would not be stopped. Within just a few months they had assumed complete control and had created an autonomous state in the region called Manchuko that they controlled with a puppet government.

And the events in Manchuria were just the beginning as the over-zealous Japanese military would not be confined to its initial expansion and in January 1932 attacked the Chinese city of Shanghai. Intent on establishing self-reliance, the military once again responded to an incident – the beating of five Japanese Buddhist monks and the burning down of a Japanese factory – with overwhelming force as some 30 ships, 40 aircraft and nearly 7000 troops were concentrated around Shanghai's coastline. Another occupation appeared imminent.

There is evidence to suggest that, like the Mukden affair, Japan's military was behind the attack on the monks and the destruction of the factory, giving them 'just' cause to lay siege to Shanghai. At first Japan issued an ultimatum to the Shanghai Municipal Council and demanded public condemnation of the beatings,

Chinese soldiers of the 19th Route Army guard a roadblock during Japan's 1932 offensive in Shanghai. ✪

compensation for property damage and visible action to suppress anti-Japanese riots that had broken out in the aftermath.

The city authorities had little option but to agree to the demands, but – because of the fractured nature of the Chinese political structure at the time – its 19th Route Army had already massed outside the city, causing consternation among Shanghai's officials and the foreign powers that had trade interests there. The move played straight into Japanese hands; aircraft from its powerful carrier fleet began a bombing campaign in response and 3000 troops quickly spread through the Chinese-controlled areas of the city. It was more than two months before China and Japan signed the Shanghai Ceasefire Agreement, and when it came it only served to put Japanese expansion on hold rather than having any power to scale it back.

While the peace would last for five years, it was a combustible situation with

Japan intent on expansion, China unable to prevent it and Japanese military leaders in the region enjoying far-reaching executive powers over the forces at their command. On the night of July 7, 1937, the two opposing forces would come face-to-face on Lugou, or Marco Polo, Bridge near Beijing and for reasons that remain a mystery there were shots fired. Both governments and international representatives moved quickly to prevent an escalation but their lack of authority over their armed forces meant there was little chance they could intervene. The situation spiralled out of control and within weeks fighting had intensified into the second Sino-Japanese War between China and Japan. With its military now even more powerful than it had been at the time of the Mukden Incident, Japanese soldiers swept down the coast with brutal consequences for Chinese troops and civilians alike and within six months Japan occupied Beijing, Shanghai and Nanjing.

Troops of the Imperial Japanese Army gather outside Mukden on September 18, 1931. ✪

RIGHT: Japanese anti-aircraft gunners watch the skies over Shanghai. Japan's Imperial Army was much better equipped than the Chinese and its greater strength resulted in a series of swift victories. ✪

Chinese civilians being prepared for burial alive under the orders of Japanese soldiers. ✪

Special landing forces of the Imperial Japanese Navy – wearing gas masks – prepare to advance in the rubble of Shanghai. ✪

Soldiers and civilians alike, the bodies of dead Chinese are piled up on the shore of the Yangtze River in Nanjing. ✪

China: The forgotten combatant

History tells us that fighting in the Second World War commenced in 1939, but that doesn't account for the two devastating years of the Sino-Japanese conflict. Japan quickly established dominance in Shanghai, but after its hard-fought victory there it showed the catastrophic nature of what was to come when its troops moved on to Nanking. With a 350,000-strong force, Japan sacked the city – it has been estimated that its soldiers tortured and murdered up to 300,000 Chinese civilians and surrendered military personnel, as well as raping tens of thousands of women during what became known as the Rape of Nanking.

China was completely unprepared for total war; it possessed little military-industrial strength, had no mechanised divisions, few armoured forces and had been in the midst of its own on-off civil dispute between nationalists and communists for decades. After heavy defeats early in the conflict, China retreated, regrouped and, despite its internal differences, managed to unite on a strategy of resistance – aiming to drag the war out as long as possible and exhaust Japanese resources while building up its own military capabilities.

By the early 1940s, Japan governed much of the infrastructure in China and occupied many of its major cities, but found controlling its vast countryside nearly impossible. As part of its resistance tactics, China engaged in guerrilla warfare and launched several ambushes and smaller attacks on Japanese forces, managing to inflict significant casualties. Frustrated by a lack of progress, Japan turned to ever-increasing levels of atrocity, launching its Three Alls Policy – kill all, loot all, burn all – and it was during this time that it carried out many war crimes including the use of chemical weapons.

Despite the continued bombardment from Japanese forces and the unimaginable loss of life China's resistance strategy – with support from the US and Russia – succeeded in preventing full-scale invasion. By the time America unleashed its new atomic bomb on Hiroshima and then Nagasaki the war was all but over, and Russian incursion into Manchuria sealed Japan's fate. After the Allied victory in the Pacific, Japanese forces in China were ordered to surrender and formally downed weapons on September 9, 1945.

While China had become a serious military power during the war, its economy had been drained having spent nearly a decade focusing all of its resources on fending off Japanese advances. The nationalist government was plagued with allegations of corruption and profiteering and, while the communists had united with their bitter rivals for the sake of

Chinese prisoners of war are executed by Japanese soldiers with bayonets in a trench during the Battle of Nanjing. ✪

RIGHT: Chinese soldiers are seen sorting grenades and ammunition.

The bombing of Chongqing was a sustained Japanese aerial campaign from February 18 to August 23 comparable to the Blitz in London. A total of 268 air raids were conducted on the temporary Chinese capital during the period with more than 5000 civilians killed in the first two days of operations alone.

On June 5, 1941, the Imperial Japanese forces flew more than 20 sorties in three hours of constant attacks during which 4000 residents were killed as a result of a mass panic – many trampled to death or suffocated in makeshift shelters and tunnels. This picture shows casualties lying in the street. ✪

Infantrymen of the Soviet Union raise the Soviet navy ensign at Port Arthur in Manchuria in October 1945. It was a symbolic act signalling the end of Japanese power in a region it had dominated since the Russo-Japanese war of 1904-1905. ✪

the war effort, the two were once again at loggerheads as to the future direction of the country and the threat of civil conflict loomed large once again.

The ravages of the war had left Chinese lands in ruins and huge swathes of farming land were unfit for purpose, leaving millions across the country facing starvation. The nationalists, already mired in controversy, were seen as a central power far removed from the destitution of rural areas. In contrast, the communists established themselves as the party of the people – particularly their leader Mao Zedong who was seen as a great leader who'd led guerrilla efforts to defend the masses during Sino-Japanese battles.

Compounding problems, the region of Manchuria once again became a central issue in postwar China. There were terrible consequences for the Japanese living there during the time of Russian occupation after the Second World War: military personnel committed ritual suicide, soldiers killed civilians rather than leave them in the hands of advancing Russian forces and those who did survive faced rape, pillage and imprisonment. Industrial infrastructure and equipment was dismantled and removed by Russia, before Manchuria was left in the hands of Chinese communists. The nationalists had agreed as part of postwar negotiations that the Russians would deal with them exclusively – but clearly the Russians had other ideas. Mao used the opportunity and moved into Manchuria – his forces arming themselves with the military hardware the Japanese had left behind – before establishing control of the countryside and moving against the nationalists in the northeast. The communist offensive was finally enough to spark war, and in 1949 the nationalists would be forced to retreat to

Taiwan with Mao proclaiming victory for the new People's Republic of China.

In the aftermath of the Second World War, the victors were able to dictate their own narrative. As the US and other Allies commemorated the terrible losses of its own peoples and promoted their own versions of events, China – whose war had been the longest and perhaps the most deadly – was largely forgotten. Its new position as a communist country made it an enemy in the over-simplistic dichotomy of the Cold War (communist bad, capitalist good), and in China itself there

A Second World War propaganda poster advocates support for China and recognition of its contribution to the conflict. Such support and any form of remembrance disappeared with the start of the Cold War and communist takeover in China. ✪

was little done to mark the impact of the war because Mao refused to acknowledge any nationalist contributions.

What it's meant is that the traditional history of the Second World War has evolved to overlook the role China played, and largely ignores the telling efforts of the steadfast Chinese resistance. First and foremost, while the Allies were struggling to hold Japan back in the Pacific, China managed to prevent complete Japanese occupation of its territory, ensuring that the Imperial Japanese Army and Navy had to divert far more time and resource to its desired conquest of the country than it had wanted. In addition, once the American war machine was up and running, China proved vital in consistently weakening Japan's position in terms of its military, industry and economy.

However, of more significant note is the tremendous numbers of Chinese casualties – both military and civilian – with estimates putting the number of dead at anywhere from 10 million to upwards of 22 million. Intense fighting, Japanese brutality, disease and famine were the main causes, with China ending the war behind only the Soviet Union in terms of total losses. Entirely unready for war and in the midst of a violent political battle that would start up again almost as soon as global hostilities ended, China seemingly had no right to fend off the Japanese for as long as it did and without its efforts and enormous sacrifice Japan's capabilities would have been significantly increased.

China's actions might not be celebrated or remembered in the same way as other history-altering events such as Midway or D-Day, but the decision of the communists and nationalists to come together and fight was perhaps just as significant on the final outcome of the Second World War.

Declaring the terms of the Washington Naval Conference obsolete, America embarked upon significant naval expansion – although it was limited by the ongoing financial crisis. New battleships USS *Washington* (pictured) and USS *North Carolina* were two examples of new vessels. ✪

The American response

Japan's swift and decisive incursion into Manchuria was exactly what the US had feared. So far the American government had managed to exert diplomatic influence over its Japanese counterparts to prevent expansion in Asia, but the Mukden Incident would soon prove that in reality it simply lacked any sufficient stopping-power.

Economic turmoil in the aftermath of the Wall Street Crash meant there was little support for financial punishment, so America sat in on League of Nations meetings for the first time to highlight the terms of the Kellogg-Briand Pact – China and Japan both being signatories of the 1928 agreement which had been reached in a bid to prevent another world war.

The invasion of Manchuria was the first major incident the pact had to contend with but, like many other treaties of the time, it lacked any means of enforcement and so was rendered largely ineffectual. With international organisations failing,

US Secretary of State Henry Stimson declared that America would not recognise the newly acquired territory as being part of Japan and rejected any actions that would impair free trade in the region. US interests in the Pacific had been growing steadily for more than half a century and trade and investment in China – and to an extent Japan – was vital to cities on the west coast and Pacific territories such as the Philippines, Guam and Hawaii. The Stimson Doctrine, as it became known, had been issued to reiterate China's territorial integrity but with no desire in America for military engagement its authority crumbled in the same way as the Kellogg-Briand Pact and the Nine-Power Treaty.

An unofficial American delegation and a League of Nations task force was sent to investigate the Mukden Incident and concluded that it had been the result of both Chinese nationalists and enthusiastic Japanese military leaders – while also

stating that the new state of Manchuko had violated the Nine-Power agreement and so would not gain international recognition. The League of Nations published the findings in 1933 and in response the Japanese delegation walked out of the council in Geneva, never to return. Soon after, Japan signed a direct truce with China that maintained its full authority over Manchuria.

The US was powerless, and was forced to accept that it now couldn't scale back Japan's expansion. Realising it needed greater military might to prevent similar situations in the future, Stimson announced that the internationally accepted Japanese disregard for the Nine-Power Treaty meant it was also no longer bound by the terms agreed at the Washington Naval Conference and so embarked on a rapid expansion of its own naval forces.

The Mukden Incident hadn't provided any appetite for military involvement in the US, but the outbreak of the second Sino-Japanese War was a much greater test of its resolve to remain isolated from such international affairs. While China would later become a communist nation, in the early 1930s it adopted many of the republican ideals that were in entrenched in the American nation and so ties between the two became ever closer. When the Japanese military began further expansion in China, and began killing civilians, public opinion turned firmly in favour of support for the besieged nation and President Franklin Roosevelt formalised aid.

There was a further souring of US-Japanese relations when the Japanese Imperial Army bombed the USS *Panay* as it evacuated American citizens from under-fire Nanjing, killing three of them. Japan issued an official apology, accepted

The Chinese delegate to the League of Nations addresses the council in the aftermath of the Mukden Incident in 1932. ✪

The Japanese embassy in Berlin, clad in the flags of the three signatories of the Tripartite Pact in September 1940 – Germany, Japan and Italy. *Bundesarchiv, Bild 183-L09218* ✳

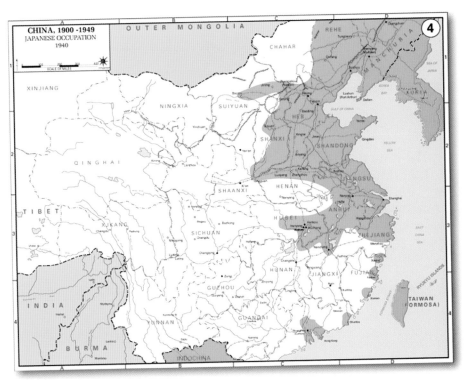

A US Army map shows the extent of Japanese expansion into China by 1940. ✪

by Roosevelt and Congress, and although an uneasy truce held, it seemed ever more likely at the start of the 1940s that America and Japan were on a collision course.

For all of its moral objections to Japanese expansion, the US also relied on Japan for income, being its main supplier of oil, steel and iron – items desperately needed by the Japanese military for its ambitious campaigns. As Roosevelt's New Deal policies took hold and military-industry in America was boosted by the sale of arms to Europe, its dependence on Japan became less important and when Japan revoked its treaty of commerce with the US, the president was able to place a restriction

on resources being sold that would benefit the Japanese military. Incapable, unwilling – or perhaps a bit of both – to stop its military, Japan's government announced it would drive western imperialists from Asia before signing non-aggression pacts with Nazi Germany, fascist Italy and the Soviet Union. The agreement with Russia caused most concern, showing that Japan had designs on moving into southeast Asia where America had an even greater number of trade and commercial interests. An additional accord with the Vichy government that now ruled France allowed Japanese troops to move into Indochina, fanning the flames even further.

It was the final straw for Roosevelt, who placed a trade embargo on Japan that deprived the nation of much-needed raw materials and created a political standoff that would never come to a peaceful resolution. The combination of the embargo, military aid flowing to China and the massing of American naval forces in the Pacific left Japan – unwilling to pull back from its commitments in China – with little option, and it would have to find a way to negate US influence. As tensions continued to simmer and negotiations failed, American military analysts alerted forces in the Pacific that a surprise Japanese assault appeared highly likely.

Japanese battleship *Nagato* and its crew in 1937. It was powerful ships like this, and their war-ready crews, that made Japan a major threat to the US in the Pacific. ✪

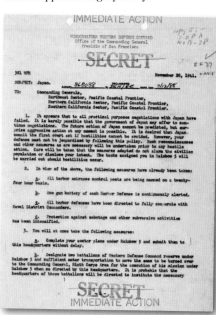

The first page of a US Army alert order, dated November 28, 1941, that was issued to commanders on the Pacific coast and in the Pacific territories indicating rising tensions with Japan could be on the verge of spilling over into direct hostilities. ✪

CHAPTER 3

The day of infamy

On the morning of Sunday, December 7, 1941 – with little warning and no time to prepare – the tranquil Hawaiian island of Oahu was transformed into the first battleground of the Pacific War as Japanese forces launched a sudden and deadly assault...

While it now seems like the obvious conclusion of a direct attack on American forces, it was never Japan's intention to engage in total war across the Pacific with the US. In fact, Japanese planning and strategy during the 1930s and early 1940s was dominated by its desire to avoid this outcome knowing it lacked the troops, equipment and resources to sustain prolonged conflict across the vast expanse of the ocean. The need for raw materials, however, was driving its Southern Expansion Doctrine – an officially adopted national policy by 1936 that called for resource-rich areas of southeast Asia to come under its authority in support of its industry, and referred to the potential of the Pacific Ocean to become a 'Japanese lake'.

Planning and preparation for a move into the area began in earnest at that time, and was initially concerned with propaganda and espionage which aimed to generate support among populations of potential foreign targets who'd lived under European rule for several generations. As the time for military action drew closer, Japanese Imperial Army leaders became ever more obsessed by the threat America posed to its grand ambitions and started to promote the idea of a preventative strike to remove the potential obstacle of an American fightback in defence of European colonies in Asia and its own territories in the Pacific. Of particular concern for Japan was how America would react to incursion into the Philippines Islands.

Leading Japanese strategists were convinced their planned operations in Asia and the Pacific would draw the US into the Second World War, but believed a carefully orchestrated strike against a prominent American target would be enough to bully the US into submission before a long and expensive conflict had time to develop. As a result, an offensive against the US Navy in the Pacific was added to the list of targets for its southern expansion, and it was the Hawaiian islands that were selected for this bold and aggressive move.

What followed was a brilliantly devised and perfectly executed military operation that would go down in history as one of the greatest tactical blunders in the history of modern warfare.

A US Martin MB-1 biplane bomber on Luke Field in August 1918. ✪

Pearl Harbor

On February 1, 1941, General Order 143 issued by the United States Navy split the US Fleet into separate Atlantic, Asiatic and Pacific Fleets. War in Europe and the need to protect convoys providing vital aid to Britain off America's east coast had precipitated the move, but it was largely driven by the desire for a significant force in the Pacific to act as a deterrent to Japanese aggression. The new concentration of ships had already been sent out into the Pacific before the fleet had been formed – undertaking war exercises near Hawaii among other exploration activities – and once the new group had been officially created the US Navy base at Pearl Harbor, on the island of Oahu, was chosen as its home.

Hawaii, particularly its sugar trade, had been an area of significant interest for expansion in the US since the mid-19th century and – with seafaring traditions dating back to America's revolutionary days – US officials also saw the Pacific islands as being an important strategic location. Following the controversial overthrow of the Hawaiian monarchy, backed covertly by US businessmen there, Hawaii became an annexed territory in 1898 and work soon began creating facilities big enough to welcome the largest American ships. Focus initially was on Honolulu, but land space was at a premium with the establishment of various US departments and bureaus – and to further compound matters it was realised that the depth of the channels there was insufficient for the more sizeable American vessels. In 1908 the decision was made to move facilities to the Naval Station at Pearl Harbor and Congress sanctioned the dredging of the channel and lochs, as well as construction of a dry dock. Within two years, four deep-sea cargo ships had docked at the new base to deliver construction materials.

Expansion of the station on the shore continued at a rapid pace in the late 1910s and early 1920s, and the US also purchased Ford Island – sitting in the middle of the bay off

Pearl Harbor – with the intention of developing both US Army and Navy aviation capabilities. The island was chosen as the location for the 6th Aero Squadron that had been formed in Honolulu in 1917, and with the US Army's development of its aerial division the region also saw the installation of improved transport networks and a civilian airport.

Housing and aircraft hangars were erected at the base itself in 1918 along with a supply warehouse, machine shop, photography laboratory and a power plant.

As US Army air operations continued, the Navy also saw the potential for Ford Island to develop into a suitable area for its own aviation activity and sought to end Army occupation – only for US Secretary of War Newton D Baker to rule that it should be divided equally between the two branches of the armed forces.

A naval air station was opened and Luke Field – the island's airstrip named after First World War Medal of Honor recipient Frank Luke – was designated for joint US Army and Navy efforts. Restrictions on expansion as a result of

the Washington Naval Conference meant there was a lull in the rapid growth at Pearl Harbor in the 1920s and early 1930s, but once Secretary of State Stimson had decreed that the US no longer had to adhere to the agreed status quo in the Pacific, building work began again in earnest. Among the changes was the addition of another airfield on the mainland – Hickam Field, opened in 1939 – that boasted a 7000ft-long runway, the only one in the region capable of use by the large bombers that had begun to dominate US Army Air Force production.

Despite the extension of Luke Field's own runway to 3000ft, the army moved its aviation divisions to Hickam as soon as the new facility was ready, leaving Ford Island under complete jurisdiction of the Navy which, under direct presidential orders to increase battle-readiness, installed an additional barracks, a new repair hangar, offices and a control tower. Domestic and leisure facilities were also built to cater for a significant jump in the number of service personnel and their families to be stationed at Pearl Harbor.

B17Ds fly over the main gate at Hickam Field, having been sent to reinforce Pearl Harbor's defences in the summer of 1941. The large bombers wouldn't have been able to use the Hawaiian island's runways before the new installation at Hickam. ✪

The impressive sight of USS *Pennsylvania* under way off New York City during American's 1934 Naval Review. But, having been commissioned in 1916, she was already close to 20 at this time and by 1941 when she was assigned to the Pacific Fleet was considered elderly. With a maximum speed of just 21 knots she would have been an easy target for Japanese submarines or air attack while at sea. The *Pennsylvania* was a symbol of how the US had neglected its military during the isolationist period between the two world wars. ✪

Neutralising the Pacific Fleet

President Roosevelt supported the recreation of the Pacific Fleet by convincing Congress to back a sizeable expansion of the United States Navy on both coasts. The fall of France to the Nazi regime in Germany demonstrated the threat the US could face on two fronts, and so the fleet's move to Pearl Harbor was supplemented by B-17 bombers, 21 one of them deployed in Hawaii from California in May 1941.

A vast naval force headed by powerful battleships and aircraft carriers had been dispatched to Pearl Harbor, joined by an Army Air Force presence consisting of 754 officers, 6706 enlisted men and 233 army aircraft – and while evidence suggests it was the sole intention of this considerable battalion to bolster Pacific defences, Japan saw America's move out into the ocean as an aggressive one.

It caused consternation in Japan's highest offices, whose officials saw the perceived American posturing as an affront. Japan knew it had the superior military – the American government having curtailed defence spending during the period of the Great Depression and deeply entrenched isolationism – but also realised that Roosevelt was rebuilding as involvement in at least one of the theatres of conflict seemed more and more inevitable. The more aggressive elements of Japanese authority believed that because they still held the advantage – for the time being – the time had come to attack.

Militarists had significant influence in Japan's government throughout the early decades of the new century, and the political climate in the country shifted completely in 1941 when hardliner general Hideki Tojo

replaced the more moderate Fumimaro Konoye as prime minister – the latter having failed in his bid to see tensions with America relieved by diplomatic means. The Imperial Japanese Army and Navy enjoyed near autocracy – demonstrated by the government's inability to scale back advances in China – and with Tojo becoming Japan's figurehead the thirst for war was only increased.

The massing of US ships, aircraft and troops at the various bases in Pearl Harbor meant it became an obvious target for a debilitating strike that would prevent American opposition to Japan's Southern Expansion Doctrine before the US had a chance to catch up with the advanced development of Japan's military.

There was a long history of army and navy rivalry in Japan but, despite there

being no love lost between the pair, Tojo turned to Japan's greatest and most-respected naval officer – Admiral Isoroku Yamamoto – who had been developing a daring plan to launch a carrier-based air attack on the Hawaiian islands.

On November 5, 1941, Tojo authorised Yamamoto's plan of attack unless Roosevelt's government accepted all of its demands in the ongoing negotiations between the two countries, and set a deadline of November 25 for a response.

America remained steadfast and so Japan progressed with its plans to seize its desired territory in southeast Asia while simultaneously launching a surprise assault that would aim to render America's Pacific Fleet useless and negate the influence of the expanded US Navy and Army Air Force bases at Pearl Harbor.

Pearl Harbor: The chain of command

Emperor Hirohito

While his influence over the autocratic Army and Navy is questionable, the Pearl Harbor military operation had to be personally signed off by Japan's head of state. ✪

Prime Minister Fumimaro Konoye

Ultimately the prime minister was responsible for overseeing international relations and Konoye favoured a peaceful solution with America. Militarists disagreed and he was ousted. ✪

Prime Minister Hideki Tojo

Army general Tojo replaced Konoye and immediately put Japan on a war footing. He even embraced the bold plans of his old rival Yamamoto. ✪

Naval Minister Koshiro Oikawa

An admiral and the main link between Japan's government and Imperial Navy, Oikawa was the first to see Yamamoto's official Pearl Harbor plan. A supporter of Konoye, once Tojo assumed power his influence was limited. ✪

Chief of Staff Osami Nagano

Japan's senior naval officer for most of the Pacific War, Nagano was against war with America and opposed Yamamoto's Pearl Harbor attack plan. He reluctantly approved when his top admiral threatened resignation. ✪

Admiral Isoroku Yamamoto

As commander-in-chief of Japan's combined fleet, Yamamoto relentlessly pursued his theory that a decisive early victory against America was required. He devised and oversaw Operation Hawaii. ✪

Vice Admiral Chuichi Nagumo

As commander of Japan's Kido Butai carrier group, Nagumo was responsible for the Pearl Harbor strike force at sea – although he was actually against Yamamoto's idea and had voiced his concerns in the months prior. ✪

Lieutenant Commander Minoru Genda

A pioneer of Japanese military aviation, Yamamoto turned to Genda for his expertise and gave him responsibility for training the required forces. ✪

Admiral Takijiro Onishi

Head of Japan's Naval Aviation Development Division in the Ministry of Munitions, Onishi played a key role in many of the technical advances that made the Pearl Harbor attack possible. ✪

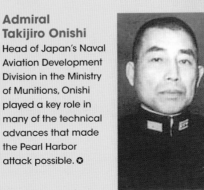

Commander Mitsuo Fuchida

Leading the first wave of aircraft, Fuchida remained in the skies over Pearl Harbor throughout the attack to offer first-hand reports on the success of the operation. He became a national hero on his return. ✪

An aerial view looking south-west across Pearl Harbor – the photograph taken on October 30, 1941. Ford Island is in the centre, with the naval yard across the channel above and Hickam Field just beyond. To the left of Ford Island is the Pacific Fleet Command Center and various other infrastructure, including fuel tanks. ✪

A new kind of warfare

America's increasing presence in Hawaii made it a viable military target for Japan, but to actually carry out a large-scale operation in the territory would take something remarkable given its distance from the Japanese islands. Pearl Harbor was out of reach for Japan's bomber aircraft, and its traditional naval strategy was that its battleship force should remain close to home waters as a defensive line rather than being an offensive group. To hit America hard enough to achieve its aims, Japan would have to come up with something truly innovative, and so Yamamoto turned his attention to the carrier fleet under his command, which was the greatest of its kind in the world.

Yamamoto had used his position and remit to promote the importance of air power at sea, and during his country's naval air exercises of 1939-1940 he was buoyed by the increased capabilities of the aircraft that had been developed and the men piloting them. The admiral had particular praise for a simulated raid on harbour-based warships by torpedo-armed bombers and, while officers and Navy Ministry officials were less convinced, he believed its success proved his theory that a carrier-based attack – as long as it had the element of surprise – could be used against the US in the Pacific.

Later in 1940, on the night of November 11 and early hours of November 12, the British Navy launched a small-scale operation from the carrier HMS *Illustrious*, with its torpedo bombers hitting the Italian battle fleet while it was moored in the southern harbour of Taranto. The result was an overwhelming victory for the British, with the sinking of one Italian battleship and heavy damage sustained by two more. The British naval officer who oversaw the campaign, Admiral Andrew Cunningham, made bold statements about the utilisation of air forces having altered naval

British Admiral Andrew Cunningham, who stated that the carrier attack on Taranto had been a turning point for navies across the world. *Dutch National Archives* *

warfare forever – a prophecy that would be realised as the Pacific War progressed.

While he was already crafting his own idea, the British success at Taranto is unlikely to have gone unnoticed by Yamamoto – the Imperial Japanese Navy as a whole certainly paid it careful attention, sending its assistant naval attaché, Lieutenant Commander Takeshi Naito, to Berlin to investigate first-hand. A Japanese military mission also visited the harbour in May 1941 for discussions with the Italian navy. In theory a carrier attack had its significant risks,

Yamamoto commanded huge respect right across the Imperial Japanese Navy, and his departure was unthinkable. As such he was able to manoeuvre Japanese thinking to suit his own aims, and his Pearl Harbor attack plan was approved. ✪

but Taranto showed that the rewards could outweigh them and when the Pacific Fleet was positioned in Hawaii it put the 100-plus-strong concentration of ships within feasible reach.

On January 7, 1941, Yamamoto formally submitted his blueprint by sending a memo to Navy Minister Koshirō Oikawa but although his plan was deemed worthy of careful consideration, it had its objectors. Devising the campaign was one thing; seeing it come to fruition was going to be an entirely different challenge altogether.

A reconnaissance photograph shows the aftermath of the British attack on Taranto. ✪

LEFT: The development of the Japanese Zero fighter – as seen here aboard carrier *Akagi* – was crucial to the evolution of the Pearl Harbor operation, and allowed Yamamoto to utilise all six of Japan's carrier aircraft for the attack. ✪

Yamamoto canvassed support, and his carrier attack plan gained backers – but the major obstacle he faced was convincing the navy's general staff that the daring raid could work alongside traditional Japanese strategy of only using its sea-going force in defence of the homelands and territorial expansion.

Even after governmental military figures had decided that an aggressive strike was needed to protect the move into the Southern Resource Area, conservative elements of the Imperial Japanese Navy were not convinced by its merit and believed that the potential for losses of its prized ships was not worth the risk when they could be used to respond to any American action from defensive positions.

Yamamoto possessed a great deal of influence in the Japanese navy, but even he couldn't just undertake a mission of this magnitude without preventing clear-cut evidence that it could work and so he began lobbying the corridors of power in a bid to see his vision come to life. He began by ordering Admiral Takijiro Onishi – chief of staff of the Eleventh Air Fleet – to study the technical aspects. His opinion was that carrying out the mission would be difficult, but not impossible. Widely respected naval aviator Commander Minoru Genda – a long-time friend and associate of Yamamoto – agreed with Onishi's findings, and once again stressed the importance of the surprise factor; such a large force so far from home and deep in enemy territory could potentially be a sitting duck if its presence was detected ahead of the final launch. Yamamoto decided to wield his authority and instructed Onishi and Genda to compile a full tactical plan and begin the training of the necessary forces. He would concentrate on the politics.

The wrangling continued into the summer of 1941 with the navy general staff expressing doubts about the operation and particularly concerned by the size of the group Yamamoto wanted to commit. A series of developments in the late summer and autumn would go in Yamamoto's favour, however – the launch of two new carriers being one important factor, and an agreement between Japan's army and navy about a staggered approach to the conquest of territory in Southeast Asia lessening the impact of such a large naval force being thousands of miles out into the ocean.

A third key event was improvements made to the engine of Japan's premier fighter aircraft, the Mitsubishi A6M Zero, that meant it was now capable of supporting Japan's southern campaign without having to be transported closer by the carrier fleet. Yamamoto had directed much resource and effort to developing Japan's naval air fleet, a decision which now made a Pearl Harbor attack much more likely.

With the barriers all but removed, Yamamoto consolidated support by spreading the word to Japanese high command that he would resign if not allowed to continue with his plan. He was his country's most decorated naval officer and a national hero who commanded the respect of the often difficult-to-control Japanese navy – his departure was not something the general staff could allow, and Operation Hawaii was given the green light.

Crew members of the carrier *Akagi* gather on the flight deck at Hitikappu Bay; at this time still unaware of the journey that awaits. ✪

A military masterpiece

Calling on all of his diplomatic experience and political skill, Yamamoto had successfully gone against decades of Japanese naval strategy to gain approval for his bold carrier strike plan – and he'd done so while simultaneously overseeing the meticulous preparation that would be needed to make it a success.

For the planning he relied on Genda, and it was his trusted commander who implemented solutions to two of the technical problems which – if unsolved – could have jeopardised the whole mission: executing torpedo strikes in the shallow harbour and making level bombing against battleships a worthwhile endeavour.

To counter these issues, Genda worked tirelessly on the development of Japan's weapons arsenal – first introducing modified torpedoes with wooden fins that prevented them getting stuck in the mud and silt of the seabed, and then instigating the development of armour-piercing bombs capable of causing massive damage even when released at a higher altitude by the bulkier level bombers.

Given the unprecedented nature of the mission they were devising, training for the attack on Pearl Harbor was also going to be crucial and once again Genda was given responsibility for this aspect. During the summer of 1941 he used Kagoshima City on the Japanese island of Kyushu – the location providing many of the same geographical elements and a similar infrastructure to those his forces would encounter upon reaching Hawaii. In training, crews had to navigate a 5000ft-high mountain before diving into the city below – avoiding buildings and smokestacks – before dropping to just a few hundred feet at the coast. There can be little doubt that the attention to detail Genda gave to the operation was crucial in helping Yamamoto convince the general staff that his plan was a viable one.

With logistics coming together under Genda's command, Yamamoto also had to contend with what was perhaps the most challenging aspect of the entire affair: maintaining the element of surprise. There were several individual parts of the operation that would make this difficult, and any one of them failing would surely have meant the plug being pulled on the overall campaign – the fact that Yamamoto was able to ensure it all succeeded was an incredible feat of military leadership and tactics. The first major obstacle to present itself was hiding the change in Japanese naval strategy from American intelligence agencies, which Japan knew were monitoring their every move.

In November 1941 Japan began a radio communications campaign aimed at tricking the US into believing that it was business as usual for the Japanese fleet – and the navy used a planned exercise to 'hide' actual radio communications to, from and between the carrier aircraft. When the radios went silent in the aftermath, America had no reason to believe that the fleet wasn't sitting in home waters in its defensive position – as had always been the case – rather than being under way and en route to attack.

Now came Yamamoto's second hurdle: ensuring the six carriers, one light cruiser, nine destroyers, three submarines and eight tankers and supply ships that had been chosen for the raid arrived undetected. From early in the planning stage, Japan had been receiving information from its agent in Hawaii on the activity of the Pacific Fleet and had been using radio intelligence to monitor air force operations. It was the latter of these that revealed a critical lack of American reconnaissance missions in the waters north of Hawaii – a Japanese offensive from this area such an inconceivable proposition that it didn't even warrant consideration.

With a northern Pacific route chosen, on November 5 the order to begin operations was delivered to senior officers and six days later Vice Admiral Chuichi Nagumo – commander of the First Air Fleet and given overall command of the Pearl Harbor strike force at sea – received the final instructions and his ships were directed to their rendezvous point in the Kurile Islands.

The main strike elements of the force, including the Kido Butai carrier battle group, departed for a position north of Hawaii on November 26, with strict radio silence observed.

With Pearl Harbor sitting at the south of Oahu and Japan's aircraft approaching from the north to avoid US patrol planes, it meant navigating Hawaii's terrain at low altitudes. This shot of Ford Island (looking north) with mountains and rolling clouds in the background shows what the pilots would have to contend with, and only when they broke through those clouds would they know whether their mission had maintained its element of surprise. ✪

Aircraft prepare to depart from the carrier *Shokaku*, while a Kate torpedo bomber is shown taking off. ✪

Japanese carrier pilots receive their final instructions ahead of the launch. ○

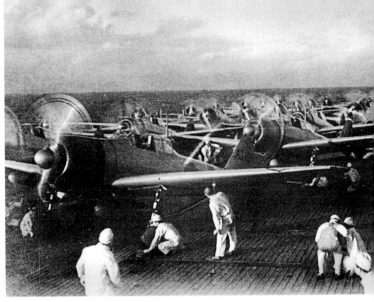

Dive bombers from *Akagi* are readied for the mission ahead. ○

Such were the efforts to maintain secrecy that only at this point were those on board given information on the nature of the mission. As the fleet moved east it was aided in its efforts to avoid detection from the sporadic US patrol planes by low cloud cover, but that brought poor weather with it and storms about 1000 miles from Hawaii had left the ships scattered across hundreds of miles of open water. In a remarkable feat of navigation, the fleet regrouped using just short-range, low-power radio.

From December 4-6, the news already having been delivered from Chief of Staff Nagano that Japan had decided to open hostilities against the United States, the strike force moved south and by the early hours of December 7 had reached a staging point just a few hundred miles north of Oahu ready to unleash the greatest concentration of naval air power ever assembled on Pearl Harbor. At 6.10am, the first wave of 183 aircraft took off from the decks of the six carriers – the incredible flock of fighters, level bombers and dive bombers launching into the Pacific skies surely ranking as one of the greatest spectacles in the history of aviation warfare – and they were just 132 miles away from their target when they were first spotted on radar.

Even then, such was the surprise factor they'd maintained that they were mistaken for a flight of American B-17 bombers which were due at Pearl Harbor that day and on approach at the time. It was only when first visual contact was made as the fighters screamed over the heads of unprepared residents of the Pearl Harbor bases that they had any notion of the impending devastation about to commence.

Devising the plan, training for it, launching it – everything had been executed to near-perfection, but perhaps the most amazing feat was that Yamamoto had managed to control the various strands of the Japanese military to ensure that the operation went exactly the way he wanted and remained a total surprise.

He had done all he could – now it was time for his strike force to launch into history and inflict as much damage on the mighty American fleet moored off the shores of Ford Island as possible.

A Japanese B5N Kate torpedo bomber crew on board the carrier *Kaga* on December 6, 1941. ○

Japanese crews cheer on the deck of *Shokaku* as a B5N Kate bomber prepares for launch. ○

The Pacific War begins

When the planes of the Japanese first wave arrived to commence their attack, commander of the air forces Mitsuo Fuchida ordered his telegraph operator to tap out "to, to, to" – the code for "attack". This was swiftly followed by "to ra, to ra, to ra" meaning "attack, surprise achieved".

Little could the pilots know, however, that although their approach to Oahu caught those at Pearl Harbor unaware, the first American shots of the Pacific War had already been fired by crew members of the Wickes-class destroyer USS *Ward*. In the calm waters around the island at 3.57am,

Ward was notified of a periscope sighting by the minesweeper USS *Condor* and she steamed out to investigate. An initial sweep found nothing untoward but then came a second sighting, this time from cargo ship USS *Antares*, whose crew radioed that they were being tailed by a non-American vessel that they likened to a mini-submarine.

The midget sub was part of the Japanese strike force, and had been dispatched to guard the entrance to Pearl Harbor and use one of the two torpedoes aboard to destroy any ships attempting to escape the air attack which was just hours away.

Such a submarine had never been seen by the crew of the *Ward* before but, following protocol despite not being totally sure what they were attacking, they duly closed in and fired guns one and three, scoring a hit with the second salvo – following that with the dropping of depth charges. News of the skirmish – which, as it turned out, was the opening act of direct American involvement in the Second World War – reached the head of the Pacific Fleet, Admiral Husband Kimmel, at the same time as the first reports of enemy planes appearing in the skies above Pearl Harbor.

The St Paul gun crew of the USS *Ward* alongside the weapon that fired America's first shots of the Pacific War. ✪

Those shots were fired against a Japanese submarine like this one which grounded at Waimanalo Beach – some 30 miles from Pearl Harbor – on December 8. One of its two crewmembers, Kazuo Sakamaki, became America's first Japanese prisoner of war. ✪

Damage from the attack's early salvos begins to show with smoke rising from land-based facilities in the background. Nearer to the camera – on board a Japanese aircraft – ripples can be seen in the water as torpedo strikes begin against Battleship Row. In recent years, it's been suggested that this photo provides evidence of a submarine-launched torpedo attack with water plumes being indicative of a submarine's propeller spray known as a rooster tail. ✪

Pearl Harbor

Two hours that changed the world

1. A Zero fighter stalks its defeated prey – a shot-down US fighter – near Oahu's Ewa Marine Corps Air Station. ✪
2. The initial aim of the Japanese attack was to prevent American aircraft from taking to the skies and launching counteroffensives. A Marine SNB Expeditor is shown burning as a result of the first-wave efforts. ✪
3. The US Army B-17E of First Lieutenant Karl T Barthelmess after landing safely near Hickam Field. His aircraft was part of a fleet of 16 bombers heading for the Philippines that arrived at Pearl Harbor for refuelling at the same time as Japanese planes were patrolling the skies. Twelve of the aircraft did attempt to touch down, and all but one were successful despite coming under heavy fire. ✪
4. The radio message sent by Ford Island Command Center. This example was received by aircraft carrier USS *Wasp* of the Atlantic Fleet. ✪
5. US Navy personnel attempt to save a burning PBY Catalina aircraft at Naval Air Station Kaneohe, east of Pearl Harbor. ✪
6. P-40 fighter planes and aircraft hangars burn at Wheeler Field. ✪

0745 |

The Japanese air attack on Pearl Harbor begins as dive bombers and fighters swarm over Wheeler Field – north of Pearl Harbor – and Hickam Field, plus the naval air station on Ford Island. The first wave aims to neutralise US aircraft, ensuring there is no chance of forces mounting a defence. With aircraft parked wingtip-to-wingtip for security, they make easy targets and significant damage is inflicted in the opening minutes of assault.

0758 |

Commander Logan C Ramsey spots a low-flying plane from Ford Island Command Center and, once he realises it's not a showboating US pilot, he orders telegraph operators to alert every ship and base with the message: "AIR RAID ON PEARL HARBOR X THIS IS NOT DRILL". Sailors and airmen, many having stumbled out of bed into the ensuing chaos, rush to their battle positions in a valiant attempt to defend Battleship Row.

0800 |

With Japanese pilots following their carefully constructed plan, the majority of American planes are unable to get off the ground – and the ones that do are quickly shot down. It leaves the skies clear for torpedo and level bombers to target the seven vessels lined up on Battleship Row and they enjoy almost instant success as an armour-piercing bomb strikes America's premier battleship USS *Arizona*, setting off more than a million pounds of explosives on board. The resulting fireball devastates the ship and within minutes she's on the bottom of the harbour. USS *West Virginia* is also hit during the initial onslaught but, with at least two bombs and seven torpedoes blowing gaping holes in her port side, it's impossible to pinpoint exactly when the damage was done.

A photographer captures the moment ammunition on the USS *Arizona* dramatically explodes, having been struck by an armour-piercing bomb. ✛

4

5

6

1. A PBY patrol bomber ablaze at Kaneohe. ✪
2. US gunners pepper the skies above Ford Island with anti-aircraft fire and flak, but it does little to prevent Japan's carefully planned and executed assault. ✪
3. Bombardment of Battleship Row continues. ✪
4. Sailors at Naval Air Station Ford Island reload ammunition clips and belts between the Japanese attack waves. ✪
5. The stricken *Arizona* is engulfed by smoke and flames which are visible for miles around. ✪
6. Thick smoke, fuelled by escaping oil, dominates the horizon as US personnel look down the channel on Battleship Row. A listing USS *California* and capsized USS *Oklahoma* are visible. ✪

0801 |

A young Japanese pilot and his wingman approach Pearl Harbor from the northwest, and they mistake auxiliary ship USS *Utah* for an American aircraft carrier. Two crews release torpedoes, and the significant strikes cause *Utah* to capsize.

0815 |

USS *Oklahoma* – positioned outboard of USS *Maryland* on Battleship Row and so bearing the brunt of Japan's overwhelming force – is another victim of the attack, and after at least five torpedo strikes the ship completely capsizes. US servicemen scramble to her upturned hull in a bid to cut out survivors – several are released, but many more are trapped below. Across the channel at the dry dock, USS *Helena* and USS *Oglala* are occupying the usual berth of battleship USS *Pennsylvania* and so are attacked by torpedo bombers.

0820 |

Already suffering "far reaching and disastrous" consequences as the result of three near-simultaneous torpedo strikes, an explosion rocks USS *California*, causing widespread flooding and fuel leaks on board the battleship. A further bomb attack causes a fire, which would take days to fully extinguish.

USS *Nevada*, having managed to get under way, beached off Hospital Point. ✪

5

6

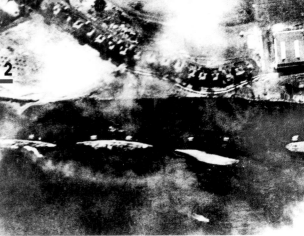

1. The scale of devastation is unprecedented, as battleship after battleship is wrecked by the Japanese onslaught. ✪
2. A Japanese aerial photograph shows the overturned USS *Utah* that had been mistaken for an American aircraft carrier. ✪
3. On the upturned hull of the *Oklahoma*, rescuers simultaneously attempt to free trapped sailors while making initial attempts to salvage the sunken battleship. ✪
4. Sailors in a motor launch pick up survivors who've been thrown into the water near the burning wreck of USS *West Virginia*, while others still aboard the ship work to save her. ✪
5. A burnt-out OS2U-2 floatplane sits among the debris on board seaplane tender USS *Curtiss* after a shot-down Japanese fighter smashed into her deck. ✪
6. USS *Raleigh* is kept afloat by barges after suffering torpedo and bomb damage. The capsized hull of USS *Utah* is visible behind. ✪

0840 |

Comprising 54 bombers, 78 dive bombers and 35 fighters, the second wave of Japanese planes arrives over the Pearl Harbor skyline.

0850 |

Among the bullets, bombs and torpedoes, USS *Nevada* attempts to head for the open sea but aircraft of the second wave bomb her. Rather than risk sinking in the narrow channel, the crew deliberately ground her off Hospital Point.

0854 |

Some US anti-aircraft gunners mount successful counter attacks against Japanese forces, but the second wave still manages to target the Pearl Harbor dry dock where USS P*ennsylvania* suffers repeated hits, as do destroyers USS *Cassin* and USS *Downes*.

The wrecks of destroyers USS *Downes* and USS *Cassin* in Pearl Harbor's dry dock. *Pennsylvania* sits just behind, with the burning *Arizona* further back still. ✪

1. Blistered paint and other fire damage suffered by USS *Pennsylvania*, which is a sitting target, being in dry dock. ✪
2. A stunning photograph captures the moment that the forward magazine of USS *Shaw* explodes, throwing debris into the air which would land up to half a mile away. ✪
3. Pearl Harbor viewed from Pier 1010: USS *Oglala* capsized in the foreground, USS *Helena* further down and Shaw burning in the background (right). ✪
4. After a brief moment of respite on Ford Island, the sailors are shocked back into action by the huge explosion on board *Shaw*. ✪
5. Smoke billows from *Shaw* behind the beached *Nevada*. ✪
6. The view from afar: *Arizona* and other ships burn in the distance as America starts the process of coming to terms with what has happened in Hawaii. ✪

0900

Having been occupied by reported submarine sightings, modern seaplane tender USS *Curtiss* turns her attention to anti-aircraft operations and manages to score a hit, only for the enemy plane to smash into her and ignite fires on board. Shortly after, a dive bomber drops its payload into the already damaged deck, setting the main hangar ablaze.

0930

Struggling to navigate the smoke pouring from the damaged ships and having to contend with anti-aircraft fire, the pilots of the second wave aren't able to inflict the same punishment as the first, but still manage to hit USS *Shaw*. A large fire rages through the ship, eventually sparking an explosion in the forward magazine – the incredible force separating the bow from the rest of the vessel and sending tons of debris into the air. Back on Battleship Row, USS *Tennessee* prepares to get under way, but is trapped among the burning wrecks of her fellow capital ships.

0945

With Battleship Row in flames and destruction spread far and wide across Pearl Harbor, Japanese fighters and bombers head back to the carrier fleet north of Oahu bringing to an end one of the most deadly and daring military operations to ever be conceived and executed.

The wreckage of a Japanese Zero fighter having crashed into a building at Fort Kamehameha – a military installation near Honolulu. ✪

A US Marine Corps sergeant at a medical dispensary the day after Japan's offensive. ✪

US Army airmen assess bomb damage at hangars on Hickam Field. ✪

While the majority of American deaths at Pearl Harbor would be military personnel, civilians were also killed during the onslaught. ✪

Bullet-ridden and burnt-out cars next to a hangar at Kaneohe. ✪

US Marines fire rifles in salute of 15 officers killed at Kaneohe during the Pearl Harbor attack. ✪

The aftermath

Confrontation between America and Japan had been brewing for years, decades – perhaps even more than half a century – yet when it finally arrived it was swift and decisive. In just two hours of blistering devastation, damage had been done that would claim the lives of 2403 Americans and leave thousands more with physical and mental wounds from which they would never recover. It was, and would remain until the terrorist attacks of September 11, the most deadly act of foreign aggression on US soil and sent shockwaves through the country that still reverberate today.

In the minutes and hours immediately following the attack, medical personnel were left desperately battling to save the lives of injured sailors and civilians – faced with the impossible situation of having to prioritise the lives of those they thought they could save over those who stood no chance of recovery. Away from the makeshift hospitals and operating theatres which had been erected to cope with the influx of patients, rescue operations continued out in the harbour as it became clear that many men had been trapped alive in the capsized or sunken ships.

Many were cut free, but despite the banging of metal being heard for days after, many more were unreachable and would be entombed in the masses of mangled ships. While the search for survivors took place, experienced commanders and officers of the US Navy acted on years of training to begin the process of salvaging the ruined vessels – many of them realising that in the shallow waters of the harbour the blows the mighty battleships had sustained didn't necessarily have to be fatal.

With the chaos ensuing in Oahu, word of the attack began to filter back to the American mainland – mainly through news radio broadcasts – where it was met with a combination of anger and resolve.

The following morning President Roosevelt made his way to Capitol Hill to deliver a speech to a joint session of the US Congress where he requested that the legislative branch formally vote to declare war on the assailants of the Pearl Harbor attack. It was during the address that he delivered what has become one of the most recognisable pieces of American rhetoric when he declared in his opening line that December 7, 1941, would be a "date which will live in infamy".

His seven-minute statement was a masterpiece of political oratory, and it had the desired effect of galvanising US public opinion behind a war that, for so long, it had been against. It seemed, initially at least, that Japan's aim of demoralising America to such an extent that it folded tamely in the face of aggression had been unsuccessful – and time would prove that this particular misjudgment was not the only one made by its military and ministerial power figures.

What Japan had achieved, however, was a stunning and categorical victory in what was the first major battle or skirmish of the Pacific War. Its aim of creating the breathing space needed for its Southeast Asia operation had also been emphatically achieved, and US forces were able to mount little in the way of defence as the Empire of Japan spent the following six months sweeping through its desired territories and occupying them with relative ease.

A dead US Navy sailor washes ashore at Kaneohe. ✪

The wreckage of *Arizona* pictured on December 10. ✪

Damaged PBY Catalinas on the seaplane ramp of Ford Island. ✿

President Roosevelt delivers his 'Infamy Speech' to a joint session of the US Congress. ✿

CHAPTER 4

The Southern Resource Area

For the first six months of the Pacific War, the Imperial Japanese Army and Navy conquered everything in their path as their forces swept down through south and eastern Asia and spread Japan's influence deep into the Pacific...

As had been its intention in the months and years of planning and preparation, and with the establishment of its Southern Expeditionary Army under the command of Count Terauchi Hisachi, the attack on US forces at Pearl Harbor was just the start of a massive operation to secure influence over vast swathes of territory in Asia and the Pacific. With China under its control to the west and having already moved into French Indochina, occupation of land to the east and south was aimed at creating an impenetrable barrier behind which the Japanese home islands would be untouchable – and from which the Empire could harvest natural resources for its ambitious expansion and huge military.

Japanese power and strength was at its peak – and while its offensive at Pearl Harbor and subsequent domination of the Allies would prove to be too great a strain on its infrastructure, during its move into the Southern Expansion Area the imperious Japanese Army and Navy would brutally conquer everything in their path.

By the end of April 1942, Japan had won every major battle its forces had entered into – and with the exception of its efforts in the Philippines they had come at a relatively low cost in terms of both personnel and equipment. Victories had seen Japanese troops occupying land – with naval influence securing the seas – from Manchuria to the East Indies, and from India's borders to deep into the Pacific.

Guam

As the only US territory in the Japanese-controlled Marianas Islands, Guam was an obvious target for the southern expansion and would form a perfect military staging area for later campaigns planned in the South Pacific as well as being an ideal strategic location in its proposed defensive belt. Wrestling the island from the Americans early in its campaign would also, according to Japan, be a hefty psychological blow to its enemy and a morale-boosting victory for its own military and citizenry.

Through intelligence-gathering efforts, the US had recognised the threat of Japanese action in Guam early in 1941 and by October had begun evacuating non-essential personnel. Given its distance from the mainland or any other major American territory, there was little serious thought given to mounting a serious defence – although the US did look to bolster the island's local militia force and provide some improvements to military infrastructure such as the naval base and seaplane facility. It would have little effect in the face of heavy aerial bombardment, however, and that's exactly what commenced just before 8.30am on December 8 – less than three hours after Guam's governor, US Navy Captain George J McMillin, had been notified by the US Asiatic Fleet that the Japanese had attacked Pearl Harbor.

Raids across the region continued throughout daylight hours until 5pm with significant damage done to the US Marine barracks, the navy yard, the local radio station building, Standard Oil Company and the Pan American Hotel. The minesweeper USS *Penguin* was also a casualty, sunk after shooting down at least one Japanese aircraft. Civilians fled the major cities, leaving them virtually deserted by the following morning when air attacks began again – with government offices and some of the island's villages added to the list of targets.

At 1am on December 10, McMillin mustered his beleaguered defence forces in the face of impending Japanese invasion but the band of 274 sailors, 153 US Marines and around 80 Chamorro troops of the native militia were no match for 400 men of the Japanese Special Naval Landing force – let alone the 5000 soldiers of the South Seas Detachment that followed. There was a short period of fighting, but on realising they were facing no more than 500 enemy fighters armed with just 12 automatic weapons between them, it soon became apparent to Japan that they had grossly overestimated the level of force required to capture Guam.

The invasion fleet assigned to the task consisted of four heavy cruisers, four destroyers, two gunboats, six submarine chasers, two minesweepers and two tenders. They therefore called a halt to hostilities and called for McMillin to cede command of the island. With complete annihilation of his troops the only other option, at 6am he issued the instrument of surrender in which he stated that the occupying Japanese had assured him that "the civil rights of the population of Guam will be respected and that the military forces surrendered to you will be accorded all the rights stipulated by international law and the laws of humanity". Guam had become the first occupied American possession during the Pacific War, and the US soldiers and sailors there were interned as the conflict's first prisoners of war.

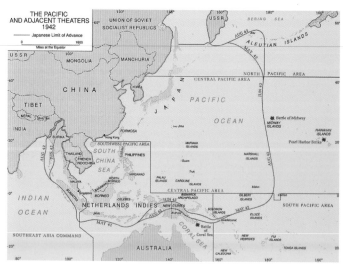

A US Army map from later in the war shows the extent of Japanese advance during its Southern Resource Area campaign. ✪

US Marines instruct Filipino cadets how to use American weapons in preparation for the imminent Japanese invasion. ✪

Japanese Type 89 I-Go tanks and troops move towards Manila. ✪

The Philippine Islands

At the start of the Second World War, the Philippine Islands were a US territory – viewed by the American government and military as a vital location given their position between the Japanese home islands and the South Pacific which included the resource-rich Dutch East Indies and Australia. While the islands weren't of enough material interest to be part of Japan's southern expansion plans originally, because of how important they were to the US they were added to the Japanese invasion plan. That importance was evidenced by the fact retired US Army general Douglas MacArthur had been called back into service by President Roosevelt and given significant finances and a fleet of 100 B-17 bombers to create a defence force – the Americans believing that a powerful aerial presence in the Philippines would deter Japanese aggression.

Given the years of underspending in the US military, however, Japan was convinced that defeat of the Pacific Fleet at Pearl Harbor would prevent the US from sending additional troops to the region and it gave Japan the confidence it needed to attack. On the same day that its carrier fleet aircraft were causing devastation in Hawaii, Imperial Japanese Army fighter planes began operations and within three days had dismantled MacArthur's air arsenal. Selected naval infantry had landed on Batan Island early in the campaign but, with air superiority achieved, it was on December 10 that the full invasion was ordered with troops offloading

on to coastlines across the island group. The combination of US Army soldiers and Filipino forces significantly outnumbered the Japanese, but they were no match for their well-trained and much better-equipped attackers, and airstrips and other key strategic facilities were quickly captured. On December 22, a total of 43,110 additional Japanese troops arrived and throughout the subsequent eight days moved south from island to island taking over cities, naval bases and airfields with ease. Each time the Japanese army secured a new location, it was able to use it as a staging area for its next advance – a carefully thought out military plan being executed to perfection. A further 7000 troops had been deployed and were moving north, the two advancing forces undertaking a pincer movement that would see them arrive in the capital Manila for a final victory.

Such was the ease of Japan's march that it pulled some of its more advanced divisions out of the Philippines campaign and their departure halted the momentum and allowed US and Filipino forces to dig in – although they were under constant bombardment from the air. While Japan had to scale back the speed of its invasion and wait for reinforcements after suffering some heavy losses, American leaders realised that continued defence of the Philippines was too costly and, with its position in the Asia-Pacific region weakening, on February 22 Roosevelt sent orders for MacArthur to leave the islands for Australia to take up the position of Supreme Allied Commander South West Pacific Area.

MacArthur had been led to believe that he would be greeted by a large US military presence on arrival, allowing him to begin operations to regain control of the Philippines almost immediately, and it led to a casual comment to journalists that "I came through and I shall return." The phrase became a rallying call of resistance on the islands with MacArthur later saying: "It was scraped in the sands of the beaches, it was daubed on the walls of the barrios, it was stamped on the mail, it was whispered in the cloisters of the church. It became the battle cry of a great underground swell that no Japanese bayonet could still." There was no army, Australia barely had the resources to defend itself, and clearly the decision had been made in Washington that – for the time being – defence of the Philippines was a futile endeavour.

US and Filipino troops did fight on valiantly, but reinforced Japanese divisions and refocused

Japanese air attacks were wearing them down – as was malnutrition and disease. Through March and April, American battalions operating on the various islands were either defeated or forced to retreat until the remaining major force of 11,000 troops were pushed back on to Corregidor – an island at the entrance to Manila Bay.

Anti-aircraft operations held off the inevitable for a short time, but in early 1942 the Japanese air command had begun installing oxygen in its bombers, meaning its pilots could reach altitudes out of range of the gunners and so heavy bombardment soon began again. Under constant attack from air and sea and with Japanese forces able to mount amphibious landings and secure strategically advantageous positions, MacArthur's replacement General Jonathan Wainwright requested terms of his surrender from Japanese counterpart Masaharu Homma.

Homma insisted that these should include the downing of weapons by all Allied forces in the Philippines – several different pockets of American and Filipino soldiers were still conducting raids on Japanese positions across the 7000-island nation.

Fearing for the fate of the inhabitants of Corregidor if he refused, Wainwright sent word to his unit commanders to surrender, and the largest of these – the Visayan-Mindanao Force – complied with the request. Many small groups and individuals refused, however, fighting on as a guerrilla resistance.

While the Philippines was the setting for the Allies' most meaningful defence against the irresistible Japanese forces at the start of the Pacific War, the losses suffered in the eventual conquest – more than 9000 killed and 13,200 wounded – makes the campaign perhaps the worst military defeat in American history.

American and Filipino troops surrender at Batan on April 9. ✪

General Wainwright announces the surrender of American forces in the Philippines on May 7, under the supervision of a Japanese censor. ✪

The British colonies

Japanese military action against American territory was concerned with neutralising US influence in the Pacific and securing positions it believed to be important in its attempts to implement de facto control of the region. Its aims to gain access to material-producing regions of Asia, however, would instead bring it into confrontation with two European nations – the first being Great Britain.

Japanese forces invaded Malaya – now Malaysia – on December 8, 1941, but because of the time difference the attack actually took place before the raid on Pearl Harbor. The outbreak of war in the Far East was something that Britain's Prime Minister Winston Churchill had feared given that his country was critically overstretched fending off the might of Nazi Germany in Africa and the Mediterranean – as well as defending its own borders from the threat of invasion.

Allied forces in Malaya – comprised of British, Indian and Australian troops – were severely unprepared and ill-equipped, yet

Stocks of rubber in Malaya are burned by the British as forces retreat into Singapore in December 1941. ○

Japanese troops advance in Malaya on bicycles. ○

offered stiff resistance against the onslaught of Japanese divisions disembarking from transport ships and coming ashore in their thousands. Japan, however, had air superiority and on December 10 demonstrated its capability by sinking both the battleship HMS *Prince of Wales* and battlecruiser HMS *Repulse* as a result of aerial bombing and torpedo attacks. It was the first time a battleship had been sunk by

enemy aircraft while under way at sea, and was a stark demonstration of the power shift from Britain to Japan in the region. Using its sea-going force to gain the upper hand in tactics and provide a constant stream of reinforcements to the land-based operation, Allied forces were driven out of Malaya as Japan set its sights on Singapore.

Britain's RAF had pinned its hopes of defending Singapore on using bases in Malaya as a staging ground, but Imperial Japanese Army divisions made that more and more untenable as they moved further and further south. By the time Japan was ready to launch against the island early in 1942, there was little left in the way of a prepared or able garrison there to defend it and the 80,000-strong force was steadily surrounded.

Lieutenant-General Arthur Percival – the British commander there – surrendered on February 15, 1942. Close to 130,000 Allied troops across Malaya and Singapore became prisoners of war, with Churchill describing the affair as the "worst disaster" in British military history. Many of those prisoners would go on to build the infamous Death Railway between Burma and Thailand – named for the high mortality rate among the labourers forced to work on the project.

Much of the blame for the capitulation was placed on Percival, but despite tactical deficiencies – not launching a counterattack when Japanese forces were close to the end

Mopping up resistance forces in Kuala Lumpur, Japanese soldiers continue their advance through Malaya. ○

While Japan's domination was undoubted, its efforts were not without casualties. Two dead Japanese troops are shown next to their destroyed Type 95 Ha-Go tank at a roadblock in January 1942. ○

Wake Island

Striving to ensure no American military force was in a position to challenge its southern expansion, Japan rolled an invasion of Wake Island into its campaign. The small atoll sits in the heart of the Pacific Ocean and at the time was home to a US Marine Corps base comprising three light cruisers, six destroyers and 450 Special Naval Landing Force troops – the proximity of the base to key Southern Resource Area targets making it a threat. The Imperial Japanese Navy made its advance on the territory on December 10, and was able to quickly eliminate its air defences – 12 Wildcat fighters – destroying seven of them before they even left the ground. American naval forces had more joy, however, and managed to repel the Japanese party, sinking two of its destroyers in the process.

The resistance would not last, and on December 23 – with the support of fleet carriers *Hiryu* and *Soryu*, which were on their way back from Pearl Harbor and had begun the launch of aerial bombing raids the night previously – 1500 Japanese troops landed on Wake and successfully forced a US submission. In total, however, Japanese losses outnumbered American deaths by more than 800 to 120 – US Marine Corps commander Major James Devereux only surrendering the island when it became clear no support from the Pacific Fleet was forthcoming.

Wrecked US Wildcat fighters at Wake Island following the Japanese invasion. ○

British soldiers push a car into the harbour at Singapore. With occupation of the city all but assured, this was part of a plan to destroy all property which might have proved useful to the Japanese. ○

Australia, Tulagi and New Guinea

In a show of striking military dominance, by mid-April 1942 Japan had achieved each of the objectives in its southern expansion campaign – and had found the Allies, America included, unprepared and poorly equipped to defend. As the early months of the Pacific War developed, countries on both sides quickly came to realise the importance of Australia.

The Allies needed it because it allowed them to continue operating trade convoys in the Pacific and was a country from which it could launch counterattacking military offensives, Japan needed to take it to prevent the Allies from turning it into a stronghold of resistance.

As the likelihood of conflict in the Pacific increased, and as war did dramatically break out, the US and Great Britain increased their reliance on the northern Australian port city of Darwin as a location from which to feed supplies to forces in the Philippines and Malaya.

With Japan progressing its invasion plan and pursuing the capture of the oil-rich Dutch East Indies, Australia became even more of a concern and, with Allies having now established a large base at Darwin, a concurrent plan was devised to launch a Pearl Harbor-style raid there.

On February 19, the Imperial Japanese Navy launched what is still the largest foreign attack against Australia when 242 carrier-borne aircraft sank 11 ships, destroyed 30 aircraft and killed 23 military personnel and civilians. A second raid came later in the day, this time executed by 54 land-based bombers from new Japanese territory in the Dutch East Indies.

Like many Japanese operations of the Pacific War's first six months, the attackers faced little opposition. Darwin was lightly defended and unable to cope with the onslaught. As the Allies regrouped and looked to establish bases at various towns and cities in the country, Japan continued its aerial assault with more than 100 raids taking place against Australia during the course of the conflict.

Despite their initial successes, Japan's military leaders were still greatly concerned by the Allied presence in Australia – so much so that the Imperial Japanese Navy's general staff recommended an invasion of the northern territory. The army rejected the measure, citing a lack of forces and shipping capacity, both of which were being stretched by large-scale operations across the Pacific and Southeast Asia.

Smoke from bombed oil storage tanks rises into the air in Darwin on February 19. The raid was Japan's first on the northern Australian port. ✪

As an alternative, Vice Admiral Shigeyoshi Inoue advocated the occupation of Tulagi in the Solomon Islands and Port Moresby in New Guinea – putting Japan's land-based bombers close enough to establish aerial dominance over Australian skies. Both the general staff and army approved the plan, and promoted the idea of further similar operations, such as the invasion of New Caledonia, Fiji and Samoa, believing it could cut off supply lines and between Australia and the United States.

In April, approval was given for Operation MO to be carried out. If successful it would see Tulagi invaded and occupied on May 2-3, followed by the invasion of Port Moresby on May 10.

A photo taken by a Japanese airman shows vessels burning in Darwin Harbour after the attack. ✪

A downed US Army Air Force P-40E, hit during one of Japan's many Australian raids of the early Pacific War. ✪

Defending Australia's northern territories and offshore locations such as the Solomons and New Guinea was going to be crucial in halting Japan's advance and eventually pushing the Imperial forces back. It was in these battles that America mounted its first successful counterattacks against Japan, such as this bombing of a Japanese airfield on New Guinea in 1942. ✪

CHAPTER 5

Critical Japanese
MISTAKES

The Pearl Harbor attack had brought together the disparate branches of Japan's military for an operationally perfect carrier raid on a never-before-seen scale that had resulted in a total victory for Japan, putting America's premier battleships out of action and neutralising the Pacific Fleet. What soon became clear, however, was that as well as inflicting a crushing defeat on US forces in Hawaii, the indiscriminate killing of more than 2000 Americans had been the act to finally wash away decades of isolationism in the US.

For all of the short-term success of the operation, as time went on it began to seem as though the act of launching it had been a miscalculation of epic proportions. The ease with which Japan found itself able to secure territory during its southern expansion brought about the stark realisation that America and her Allies had been entirely unprepared to face such an assault and were unwilling to commit additional forces to stop it even when they had realised what was happening.

The need for a pre-emptive strike on the US Navy, it became clear, had been grossly overestimated. In Japanese military planning, the desire to begin operations against the US in the Pacific was driven

As Japan's Empire swallowed up territory after territory, it became clear that there were some crucial weak spots that could prove costly; and the speed at which it achieved its expansion only magnified its earlier mistakes...

by an ironclad belief that its southern expansion would draw such ire from Washington that it would bring the US into the theatre of war. The major worry for the Japanese, and Yamamoto in particular, was America's huge industrial advantage. The Americans had to be prevented from bringing this to bear at all costs.

Yamamoto had plenty of evidence to support this belief, having been the senior naval attaché to Washington between 1926 and 1928, and spent many months of his time stationed there travelling the country and developing his understanding of America and its culture – particularly its business and economy. History has shown that his fears – and those of Japan more generally – were certainly warranted, but what Yamamoto and fellow strategists had spectacularly misjudged is how far they could push before the US fought back.

Unbeknown to Japanese military planners, the US navy had decided against a counter-offensive charge across the Pacific as early as 1935 – part of its evolving Plan Orange designed to deal with the potential of war with Japan that was developed between the First and Second World Wars. American leaders had instead decided to commit to keeping the Imperial Japanese Navy out of the eastern Pacific – a key reason behind its decision to relocate the Pacific Fleet to Hawaii. They had also decided that protecting shipping lanes to Australia was vitally important.

These two defensive aims were to be pursued while the US concentrated on the expected conflict with Germany; Nazi leader Adolf Hitler did indeed declare war on America on December 11 in response to what he claimed to be a series of provocations by the Roosevelt administration that was supposed to still be neutral. While Japan had no way of knowing it, the need for a strike against America to prevent the Pacific Fleet launching in an aggressive challenge to its southern expansion had evaporated. What Japan had also failed to recognise was the

widespread isolationism movement in the US that had been and remained a driving force behind War Plan Orange.

Having established and maintained its desire to be removed from international affairs since the first days of its independence, American foreign policy had evolved over the years and decades to include a degree of imperial ambition – but its unwillingness to become embroiled in global conflict was still entrenched, and had only hardened after it had made an exception to provide support in Britain and France during the First World War.

President Woodrow Wilson had advocated an international role for America in the 1920s after his decision to commit forces to Europe, but the hawks in Congress had rejected involvement in the League of Nations and the US continued to remain militarily isolated from the growing crises across the Atlantic and Pacific, even with the beleaguered Allies suffering at the hands of Germany and with Chinese civilians being brutalised and killed by the invading Japanese.

The occupation of Paris was seen by many in America as a final straw – the US and France having long-standing ties going back to their respective revolutionary days – but still Roosevelt could not generate the support to engage. Perhaps it was the contrast in the styles of government – Japan led by its authoritative military while the US operated with its three branches and checks and balances – but senior Japanese officials just couldn't seem to grasp how much power the notion of isolationism possessed.

In what was arguably its most critical error of the Pacific War, the spectacular deployment of Japan's carrier fleet to strike a blow against Pearl Harbor – rather than just chipping away at less-important US outposts – provided the catalyst to end isolationism and created an environment that unleashed America's vast military-industrial strength; precisely what Japan had intended to prevent.

Feeling towards war in America changed dramatically after Pearl Harbor, and it generated a propaganda campaign that called for retaliation. ✪

A delayed declaration

By attacking the Pacific Fleet at Pearl Harbor, Japan wanted to test America's resolve for war but, in attempting to demoralise the US and turn public opinion even further against conflict, the death and destruction it wreaked had the opposite effect – as did the way in which it went about declaring hostilities open.

Throughout 1940 and during the breakdown in relations between the two countries, America and Japan had continued negotiations – sometimes sporadically – in an attempt to avoid a war that neither really wanted. For the US this was a collective effort of its government, but it was more complex in Japan where army and navy officials wanted talks to continue as a ruse in case of attack while government officials had a genuine desire to see a diplomatic resolution. During his planning of the attack, Yamamoto agreed that it should appear as if Japan was aiming for a peaceful conclusion – even when it became apparent that would not happen – but he also stressed the importance of an official declaration of war prior to the first bombs dropping in accordance with international law. As with many other elements of the operation, Yamamoto got his way.

With Tojo's elevation to prime minister, Japan's military moved on to the front foot and – after US Secretary of State Cordell Hull delivered the news to Japanese ambassador Kichisaburo Nomura on November 26 that any accord between the two countries must include the withdrawal of troops from China – his country began work on a 5000-word transmission intended to be a pre-attack declaration of war.

As the Japanese carrier fleet approached its staging point north of Hawaii, Tokyo began transmitting the message to its embassy in Washington with the intention of it being delivered to Hull at 1pm – 30 minutes before the offensive was due to begin. In the meantime, American codebreakers had begun deciphering the Fourteen-Part Message – so named because

Americans in New York City's Times Square take in the shocking news that their country has come under surprise attack from Japan. ✪

it was sent and translated in 14 parts – and began to understand the nature of its contents the more they revealed. Crucially, however, when the 14th part was uncovered it made no official mention of war, instead just stating that: "The hope to preserve and promote the peace of the Pacific through cooperation with the American government has finally been lost". The internationally accepted Hague III Convention on the Opening of Hostilities stated that they should not begin "without previous warning" and that either an unconditional declaration of war should be made, or a conditional declaration coupled with ultimatums. The Fourteen-Part Message made no such demands.

As 1pm in Washington approached, Nomura delayed his meeting with Hull by 45 minutes – eventually being received by the US Secretary of State at 2.20pm. The fact that Nomura placed the translated document in the hand of Hull nearly an hour and a half after he was meant to was crucial because, at the time of the supposed declaration, Pearl Harbor was already under

Japanese ambassador Admiral Kichisaburo Nomura (left) and special envoy Saburo Kurusu (right) continue their negotiations with US Secretary of State Cordell Hull (centre) on November 17, less than a month before the Pearl Harbor attack. ✪

attack. The delay was attributed to Japan's late decision to deliver the information in Washington rather than at the US embassy in Tokyo, and because of how long it took Japanese officials in the American capital to decode and then translate the communication. Due to how important the elements of secrecy and surprise were to the Pearl Harbor attack, speculation persists that Japan's far-reaching military deliberately prevented an explicit declaration of war and then made concerted efforts to ensure it arrived late.

Instead, or as well, it's also believed that there was an element of incompetence on the part of Japanese officials in their efforts to relay the declaration on time. The truth of the matter probably lies somewhere in the middle, but whatever the reasoning the results were that Japan had contravened international law and launched what Roosevelt characterised as a sneak attack. It was just further fuel added to the fire that gave rise to an angry and vengeful America, rather than the demoralised opponent Japan had been aiming to create.

The headline of the *Gettysburg Times* on December 8 outlines the 'deception' of Japan's controversial declaration of war. ✪

US aircraft carriers

A further failing in Japanese thinking was that Yamamoto, and other naval leaders, did not recognise that aircraft carriers had now replaced battleships as the most powerful and threatening element of a navy's arsenal. It was certainly an ironic mistake, given that Yamamoto was such as proponent of carrier warfare and had used his own fleet to such devastating effect at Pearl Harbor.

Just to accentuate the point, it was actually one of the few errors to occur during the operation in Hawaii which demonstrated just how important carriers had become; owing to poor intelligence gathering the three American carrier vessels of the Pacific Fleet – USS *Lexington*, USS *Saratoga* and USS *Enterprise* – were all absent from their berths at Ford Island on the morning of December 7 and so escaped the fate suffered by US battleships.

In the precarious months that followed Pearl Harbor when the Allies were left reeling by Japanese advances, US carriers – particularly given the lack of battleships – provided stern defence and conducted several raids against Japanese-held islands. While they may not have done much to halt Japan's advance, they did hold up the enemy at times, sap resources and inflict losses – none of which it could afford given its desperate need for raw materials.

The full impact of Japan's inability to take out the Pacific Fleet carrier force at Pearl Harbor was being felt and it would go on to be a key element of its eventual defeat – as would the decision to omit infrastructure from its list of targets.

The USS *Lexington*, one of America's aircraft carriers which was absent from Pearl Harbor on the day of the attack. Given the role they would play throughout the Pacific War, and with the advancements made in naval aerial combat, it proved to be a huge mistake that they weren't affected by the events of December 7. ✪

Given its confidence that the destruction of the American battleships would bring a swift victory or force the US to back down, Japan neglected the ship repair yards, oil tank farms (which were already being moved because of American fears about their vulnerability), the submarine base and command buildings. None of these areas were part of Yamamoto's or Genda's plan of attack, yet they would all go on to prove more pivotal to America's war effort than any of its battleships.

In the aftermath of the Pearl Harbor attack these crucial mistakes were not immediately recognised, but as the repercussions began to be felt questions were asked of Yamamoto and others involved in the operation – and it was during this time that the notion of an abandoned third wave attack emerged.

There's little evidence to suggest that an impromptu extension to what was already a complex military mission was ever seriously considered in the midst of the action – a lack of fuel, the absence of a surprise element, the issues of extending the operation meaning returning aircraft may have to land on the carriers after dark and fears that American aircraft carriers could be within range for a counterattack all significant factors. It's believed, however, that Yamamoto later lamented Nagumo's decision not to launch a third strike against dockyards and other such facilities and it was reported that both Genda and Fuchida had both urged further action at the time.

Pearl Harbor's fuel storage tanks (left) and submarine base (right). Had they been targeted and destroyed during Japan's attack, America's ability to operate in the Pacific could have been impaired for a year or more. ✪

Carrier USS *Yorktown* preparing for Pacific operations at Pearl Harbor in May 1942. ✿

A grand final battle

A key component of Yamamoto's Pearl Harbor plan – and the reasoning behind the decision to proceed with the attack despite US aircraft carriers not being there – was his belief in the doctrine of influential naval strategist Alfred Thayer Mahan, author of the 1890 book The Influence of Sea Power Upon History: 1660-1783.

Mahanian theory was widely adopted by all the major navies of the time, but Yamamoto was a particularly avid subscriber to his arguments that supremacy at sea comes from the number and strength of a nation's capital ships – namely, its battleships. Technology had advanced significantly in the time since Mahan's work had been published but Yamamoto – even though he himself had been a key player in the development of aerial capability at sea – remained convinced that battleships were key and had begun to stockpile them in anticipation of an American incursion into Japanese waters.

His aim there – also in keeping with Mahan – would be to win a great victory in a definitive final clash where battleship took

on battleship, and it was his prophecy that war with America would be decided in this way that inspired his attempts to weaken or destroy the Pacific Fleet battle force in Hawaii. He either wanted to avoid the need for great battle, or ensure Japan held the advantage if it came. Instead, because Japan had simultaneously rendered US battleships ineffective and sparked the total war it wanted to avoid, America had to rely on its carrier force which was able to use its aerial attackers to remain a good distance away from enemy cruisers and battleships while launching its raids.

Yamamoto and other Japanese leaders were convinced that victory – perhaps even survival – depended on forcing one of its major enemies out of the war, and following its early domination waited in hope that either the United States or Great Britain would look to negotiate an armistice or peace treaty. No such concession was forthcoming. With the notion of an Australian invasion already having been rejected and no genuine chance of moving from Burma into India, attention turned

back to America and the Pacific. A blockade of Australian ports – another Mahanian theory – would do damage, but Yamamoto pushed once more for his much-coveted decisive final battle and began to hastily draw up plans to lure the remainder of the Pacific Fleet including the aircraft carriers into open water by launching an invasion of Midway Island.

While not vital to Japan's aims, Yamamoto reckoned the tiny atoll to be of strategic importance to the US as an outpost for Pearl Harbor – it being about 1300 miles north-west of Oahu – and it had been earmarked by America as a perfect location for submarine and seaplane bases. Japanese naval general staff were reluctant to back Yamamoto, given that American aggression had not been suppressed by the Pearl Harbor attack, but the sensational and successful effort by the US to bomb the Japanese home islands incensed its army and navy high command to such an extent that it gave its backing for the Midway operation. Little did they know that the fleet was being sent into an American ambush.

The US base at Midway Island. Yamamoto correctly believed it to be of vital importance to US Pacific strategy, and deduced that an invasion of the atoll would bring America's carrier fleet into the area, allowing Japan to secure a decisive final victory. ✪

CHAPTER 6

Reaction and retribution

The attack on Pearl Harbor put a decisive end to all doubt and indecision for the US, after nearly 165 years of being torn between isolationism and the desire for a global role. It entered the Pacific War infused with a new sense of common purpose that crossed all social and political divides...

Uncle Sam was used to encourage Americans to join the US Army, but in the immediate aftermath of Pearl Harbor such campaigns proved unnecessary as US citizens headed to recruitment centres in their droves. ✪

A mid the euphoria and celebrations in Japan after the Pearl Harbor attack, Admiral Isoroku Yamamoto alone is supposed to have expressed his reservations with the famous line: "I fear all we have done is to awaken a sleeping giant and fill him with a terrible resolve."

There is no written record of him actually having said this – despite actors portraying him in two of the major Hollywood films on the subject giving voice to it. Yet there can be no doubt that the attack and its aftermath left Yamamoto feeling increasingly uneasy. In spite of all the efforts he had exerted to see his grand plan come to life, he was fundamentally against provoking conflict with the United States – in fact he was opposed to overt Japanese aggression and military engagement as a general rule.

A product of Japan's less conservative pre-First World War institutions, Yamamoto favoured a far less belligerent approach to securing a global role than was being pursued by the Imperial Japanese Army and was a public critic of the strong rhetoric and overzealous use of force by the military. His views had come to the fore in the 1930s as he voiced opposition to Japan's actions in Manchuria, its conquest of China – and as Navy vice minister from 1936-1939 he made deliberate moves to stall Japan's alliance with Nazi Germany.

His rejection of what was by now a popular nationalist movement in Japan saw him firmly in the minority, but Yamamoto was absolute in his belief that America was an enemy not to be angered – an assessment he'd formed during his extensive travels to the country during his time as naval attaché in the 1920s. He had seen the vast industrial potential, the domestic supplies of oil, the factories, the modern cities, the agricultural heartlands – he knew that if those resources were focused on a war effort it could end not just with Japanese defeat, but with its complete annihilation.

He was also adamant that Japan's continued volatility in Asia would be the provocation he so feared and bring a reaction from across the Pacific. When the US embargoed oil exports to Japan he was proved correct.

Feeling that his country was drifting aimlessly to a war of attrition it simply had no chance of winning, Yamamoto decided the time had come to roll the dice and ramped up preparations for his carrier attack. Conflict was inevitable, and he would do everything in his power to give Japan an advantage from the outset.

His aim to earn a decisive early victory was a calculated gamble fraught with risks, and it had failed. The Pacific Fleet battleships might have been severely damaged, and the Japanese military might have been conquering everything in its path in Asia and the Pacific territories, but back on the American mainland Yamamoto's biggest fears were being realised as a nation dramatically mobilised for war.

Having spent many years in the country, Yamamoto knew that if America could unlock its vast industrial potential for the benefit of war then its enemies could never win a conflict of attrition. He's pictured (far left) in February 1926 during his time in Washington, DC as naval attaché with US Secretary of the Navy Curtis D Wilbur, a fellow Japanese naval officer and Admiral Edward W Eberle – the chief of US naval operations. ✪

Reaction

The response of the American public to the events of December 7, 1941, was unprecedented. Until that time its citizens were accustomed to isolationism, the government representing them insistent on remaining detached from the entangling affairs of Europe and with no real desire to become physically involved across the Pacific. Day-to-day lives in America – particularly in the immediate past owing to the hardships of the Great Depression – were concentrated on self-sufficiency and local issues; there was no far-reaching collective national movement of any note, let alone one that promoted the idea of America flexing its military muscles. By the morning of December 8, there had been a remarkable and widespread U-turn.

Almost overnight came a sweeping effort by nearly all pockets of American society to not only prepare for total war but inflict a crushing defeat on any foe that might dare to stand against it. Since Roosevelt's tenure in the White House had begun he had pursued and implemented a series of policies known as the New Deal – his attempt to get the US working again after the desperate years in the immediate aftermath of the Wall Street Crash. Among the string of new laws, enacted programmes and executive orders, Roosevelt inspired several new projects to improve American infrastructure and put American workers in jobs on a government wage.

His efforts certainly brought much-needed relief, and the nature of the work being undertaken – hydroelectric and irrigation, road building, railway upgrades, rural electrification, plus the modernisation of the telephone, water supply and oil pipelines – brought the US close to being the most advanced industrialised nation in the world. But, such was the impact of the Great Depression, it had still not done

enough to fully bring the country out of its slump; America had the capacity, but lacked the demand. The onset of war would change that dramatically.

With isolationism wiped away in one fell swoop, America focused both its capitalist system and government-backed industry on the task of securing victory. Having already begun sending resources and equipment to Britain and China through Roosevelt's various executive initiatives – needed to circumnavigate isolationist opposition – the US was now able to officially assume the role of the world's biggest supplier of oil, timber, steel, copper, aluminium, plastics, rubber and food, and the exporting of these items provided a welcome additional stimulus to the domestic rebuilding programmes. Given the significant under-funding which had occurred in the US military in the years between the two world wars, there was also an immediate need to produce more vehicles and equipment – particularly aircraft.

By January 16, 1942 – a little more than a month after Roosevelt had demanded a declaration of war against Japan in Congress – he had established the War Production Board (WPB) agency to supervise America's industrial efforts. The body was responsible for directing the conversion of all US manufacturing from peacetime work to war needs, and lead the campaign to source and distribute the materials required. Even before the

The US Office of Price Administration ordered the rationing of tyres in January 1942 after the fall of the Dutch East Indies – a key producer of rubber. ✪

WPB had been appointed, the US Office of Production Management had dictated Detroit's Big Three automakers (General Motors, Ford and Chrysler) to cease making cars and start building planes – and in a matter of weeks it was happening, the firms beginning to produce aircraft parts.

It was a scene mirrored across the country; silk factories turned to parachute production, other car plants made tanks, typewriter companies began making machine guns, clothing manufacturers sewed mosquito netting – a rollercoaster manufacturer even converted its operations to producing bomber repair platforms. The nature of industry in America had changed, and it was reflected in the numbers; with the early focus being aircraft production the

B-24 bombers under construction at Ford's Willow Run line. The manufacturing of military aircraft replaced civilian car production as emphasis shifted to the war effort. ✪

M3 General Grant tanks being built at the new Chrysler Tank Arsenal. ✪

Second World War aircraft production (all types)

	1939	1940	1941	1942	1943	1944	1945
United States	2141	6068	19433	47,836	85,898	96,318	46,001
Great Britain	7940	15,049	20,094	23,672	34,900	40,300	20,900
Russia	10,382	10,565	15,737	25,436	34,900	40,593	20,900
Germany	8295	10,862	12,401	15,409	24,807	40,593	7540
Japan	4467	4768	5088	8861	16,693	28,180	8263

Factory workers assemble B-25 bombers at North American Aviation in Kansas City in October 1942. ✪

US Second World War military production totals

Battleships	10
Aircraft carriers	27
Escort carriers	110
Submarines	211
Cruisers/destroyers/escorts	907
Railway locomotives	7500
Guns and howitzers	41,000
Landing craft	82,000
Tanks and armoured vehicles	100,000
Ships (of all type)	124,000
Aircraft (of all type)	310,000
Steel production (tons)	434,000
Vehicles (of all type)	2,400,000
Rifles and carbines	12,500,000
Cotton textiles (yards)	36,000,000,000
Rounds of ammunition	41,000,000,000

Source: The National WWII Museum, New Orleans

US went from having a total of 6000 units produced in 1940 to 85,000 in 1943. It was manufacturing on a scale that had never been seen before in history, and America's already-stretched enemies had little chance of keeping up.

While the physical results of America's rapid increase in industrial production were impressive, perhaps just as remarkable, if not more so, was the culture change that accompanied it. Before Pearl Harbor the Pacific Theatre wasn't something on the minds of many Americans, and while the newspapers kept events in Europe on the public mind there was no genuine concern about the potential for American involvement. Now, in a radical reversal, America became obsessed with the war effort and everything was approached from a viewpoint of 'what can I do to help?'

The pioneering American spirit that had fuelled its westward expansion a century earlier was reinvigorated. Not only were US citizens driven by the desire to defend their own way of life, but the old ideals of Manifest Destiny returned and Roosevelt encouraged the idea of America as the arsenal of democracy that would bring its values of freedom and independence to a wider world that was being engulfed by fascism. This was supported by a constant stream of propaganda in print media, and there were scarcely any movies produced where the plot wasn't concerned with America's role in the war and the world it was being fought in.

Civilians bought into the new wartime culture in their millions, and several thousand flocked to army sign-up centres in the immediate aftermath of Japan's assault on Oahu, outraged at the sneak actions of their eastern enemy. For many of those who would be staying in America, the wartime changes brought opportunities that had not existed since before the Great Depression and this is evidenced by the fact that the US reached full employment during the period of its involvement in the global conflict. Factories hired as many hands as they could, simplifying tasks and providing training so even the least-skilled of American workers could contribute.

Women at work on a bomber at Santa Monica's Douglas Aircraft Company. ✪

With the eventual number of servicemen away from home reaching 12 million, new sources of labour were required and so factories reached out to women and racial minorities who had previously faced many barriers that prevented them from entering the workforce. Increased manufacturing bought with it some of the best economic conditions America had enjoyed for decades and income equality reached a peak during the war – and for many years after.

It meant that even though unimaginable hardships were occurring overseas, the standard of living in America was maintained and even improved. This was particularly important in promoting military involvement because although those signing up would be risking their lives – and there were many that would never return – many of those that survived the fighting would be coming home to a much better life than the one they had left and were guaranteed education, housing and employment assistance thanks to such legislation as the Servicemen's Readjustment Act of 1944, known commonly as the GI Bill.

PLEASE DRIVE CAREFULLY. MY BUMPERS ARE ON THE SCRAP HEAP

Hollywood movie star Rita Hayworth sacrificed her bumpers for the duration of the war, setting the example of turning in unessential metal car parts – just one of the major national campaigns that civilians undertook with great pride and endeavour. ✪

USS *Oklahoma* righted to about 30 degrees on March 29, 1943. ✪

A floating crane removes the sunken mainmast from USS *California* while she is under salvage in February 1942. ✪

Divers of the Salvage Division emerge from a gas-filled compartment aboard one of the vessels damaged during Japan's attack on Pearl Harbor. ✪

Pearl Harbor: Recovery and salvage

Captain Homer N Wallin (left) – in command of the Salvage Division – and *West Virginia* commanding officer Lieutenant Commander White on board the ship while it was under salvage. During repairs on the ship, workers found the bodies of 66 crew who'd been trapped below in the only remaining air bubble among flooded areas of the ship. Three were found in a storeroom compartment where it was presumed they had survived for a time on emergency rations including fresh water – and a calendar indicated that they were still alive as late as December 23. ✪

Epitomising the industrious and determined attitude that swept across America in the aftermath to the Pearl Harbor attack were the actions of those stationed and living at its bases. Many of the servicemen targeted by Japanese forces that day would never have seen active service – and certainly not on the scale of devastation, death and destruction that was experienced on December 7. Yet in the face of such adversity, the mood on Oahu – sombre though it might have been – mirrored what was happening on the mainland and all facets of life both military and civilian were refocused to be as efficient as possible for the war effort.

An area where this shone through brightest was in the attempted salvage of the stricken ships of the Pacific Fleet. In the weeks following Japan's raid, the Pearl Harbor Navy Yard – so inexplicably excluded from the list of targets – went to work, and by February 1942 had put three battleships (USS *Pennsylvania*, USS *Maryland* and USS *Tennessee*), three cruisers (USS *Honolulu*, USS *Helena* and USS *Raleigh*), two destroyers (USS *Helm* and USS *Shaw*), seaplane tender USS *Curtiss*, repair ship USS *Vestal* and the facility's floating dry dock either back into service or ready to steam to the mainland for final repairs. *Raleigh* and *Shaw*, the most damaged of this group, were both back in

active duty by the middle of the year.

Work on the remaining ships – those which were sunk or damaged enough to face the possibility of write-off – was also under way, led by a formal salvage organisation under the jurisdiction of Captain Homer N Wallin who was previously a member of the Pacific Fleet Battle Force staff. With so many ships out of action and America working to improve its forces before making moves against Japan in the Pacific, many US Navy crewmen in Hawaii were assigned to the new Salvage Division and in the weeks after the attack they began the monumental job of putting the remainder of the mighty Pacific Fleet back into action.

USS *Nevada* was re-floated in February 1942, USS *California* a month later and USS *West Virginia* in June – and as a result of extensive shipyard repairs back on the west coast these three vessels were all back in action in time to take part in Pacific War operations. USS *Oklahoma* was subject to an extensive salvage effort that involved turning her upright and patching gaping holes in her hull, but such was her condition and age that it was deemed too costly to return her to duty. The same righting equipment used to roll *Oklahoma* was employed on USS *Utah* – but although some consideration was given to refloating her, because she'd only been used as a target and training ship it soon became clear that

A view of USS *Arizona's* superstructure shows the extent of the damage she suffered. It was soon realised that *Arizona* was beyond salvage, but much of her equipment could be rescued and reused. ✪

USS *West Virginia* – one of the ships which bore the brunt of Japanese attacks on December 7 – prepares to enter the dry dock at Pearl Harbor Navy Yard just a little more than six months after America's 'day of infamy'. ✪

Three US Navy sailors watch on as USS *Nevada* departs Pearl Harbor on April 19, 1942 – presumably for a trial run – following her initial salvage. Three days later she would steam to Puget Sound Navy Yard for permanent repairs and modernisation. ✪

An aerial view of *Arizona's* hull from the 1950s. It was during this time that the US Navy approved its use as a permanent memorial to the victims of the Pearl Harbor attack, and work began on a public viewing platform. ✪

the work needed would be too extensive and expensive. Once, *Utah* was partially upright she was moved away from the busy shipping channel closer to Ford Island where she remains today.

Another ship beyond rescue was USS *Arizona* and although some thought was given to removing the intact portions of the vessel in order to refloat the main hull, once divers had examined the wreck it was soon realised that the damage inflicted

had been far too great for salvage to be an option. During 1942, *Arizona's* guns were removed along with the majority of her superstructure that still sat above the water line. The rest was left where it sank, becoming a tomb for more than a thousand sailors who had perished on board. After the conclusion of the Pacific War the wreckage became the site of a permanent memorial to her casualties and those killed at Pearl Harbor.

By the time the Salvage Division was disbanded, US Navy and civilian divers had spent close to 20,000 hours underwater from a total of 5000 dives, and there had been exhausting efforts to recover human remains, documents, ammunition and other items and equipment from oil-filled ships that had been submerged for months. It represented one of the great salvage campaigns in history, and became a symbol of America's resilience.

With their orders in hand, Captain Marc A Mitscher – skipper of the USS *Hornet* – chats with Army Air Forces attack leader Doolittle. The ground-breaking attack by land bombers launched from carriers was the result of a collaboration between the branches of the American military. ✪

Retribution

An embarrassing and ill-fated campaign to defend the Philippine Islands from the Japanese, and continued failures to protect Allied territory in Asia and the Pacific, prompted the American people to question the government and military. The new-found enthusiasm for war wasn't just manifesting itself in industry – civilians and military personnel alike had a thirst to see decisive American action.

Roosevelt had little intention of committing troops to the war before he felt prepared to do so but, seemingly unable to lay a hand on the enemy as they expanded southwards, he shared the public's desire to strike a blow and demonstrate that America was very much still in the contest. Setting aside his long-term aims to bolster his military and launch a slow and measured fightback across the Pacific, before 1941 had ended the president had ordered his joint chiefs of staff to devise a plan for a bombing raid on the Japanese home islands.

With American bases in the Pacific being systematically captured by the Japanese, and no carrier-based aircraft capable of delivering a significant enough payload for the job at hand, there appeared to be no way in which US forces could reach their intended destination. That was until a chance observation by Navy captain Francis Low, who saw land-based American twin-engine bombers take off from a runway that

Doolittle wires a Japanese medal to a bomb so it can be returned "with interest" to the military forces which originally awarded it. ✪

had been painted with carrier markings for other aircraft types to practise landings on. He reasoned that if they could take off within the length of a carrier deck painted on the ground, they could take off from the deck of a real carrier. It was a theory

he passed on to Admiral Ernest J King, appointed as US Fleet Commander-in-Chief in December 1941.

Encouraged by the idea, King and US Army Air Forces leader General Henry H Arnold assigned aviation maverick Lieutenant Colonel James H Doolittle to organise and lead the daring mission and the new but well-tested North American B-25B Mitchell medium bomber was selected as the aircraft he would use. Doolittle started to enlist volunteer air crews for what was at the time an unspecified mission, and began an intensive training programme while also making several modifications to the B-25Bs including the removal of their defensive guns to save weight and the addition of extra fuel tanks for an extended range.

At Eglin Field in Florida, Doolittle installed catapults at shortened airstrips and had his pilots take off in as short a distance as they possibly could; landing, however, was not practised. It had been deemed impossible to achieve and instead the bombers would fly to friendly territory in China. Even with the gruelling training coming to an end, the Army Air Force pilots were still not told of their targets, but when they were given navy etiquette lessons rumours began to swirl among the group that they would be striking somewhere in the Pacific – most speculating that the

A photograph from another ship of the task force puts into perspective the size of the aircraft against the launch vessel and shows the enormity of the task that Doolittle faced ensuring the bombers could take off. It also demonstrates the heavy seas at the time of take-off, although this was used to the crew's advantage with a Navy launching officer timing the start of each bomber's take-off to ensure that it reached the forward end of the flight deck as the carrier pitched up therefore giving extra lift at the critical moment. ✪

US Army Air Force crew load ammunition into the bombers on the deck of *Hornet* while en route to a position off the coast of Japan. ✪

Philippines was the intended destination. Doolittle ordered the men at his command to end their speculation and keep their mouths shut, concerned that word of the audacious operation could leak.

By April 2, 16 B-25Bs had been loaded on to the flight deck of the aircraft carrier USS *Hornet* and she headed west across the Pacific to meet up with fellow carrier USS *Enterprise* which would provide air cover during the approach to the planned staging point some 400 miles from Japan. It was during this time that Doolittle revealed

the primary target of the mission would be Tokyo – and it was a statement that elicited jubilation from the crew who cheered the news. Doolittle asked if any of the selected pilots wished to swap with reserve airmen and navy aviators offered up to $150 to take their place, but none accepted.

As the details of the mission spread through the ship, a handful of officers who had been decorated in Japan during peacetime cooperation tied their medals to the bombs – the payloads subsequently loaded onto the aircraft in preparation

for the launch that was scheduled for the afternoon of April 18.

Shortly before dawn, however, the taskforce encountered enemy picket ships that had ventured much further east than expected and while all were evaded or sunk it was believed that they had managed to send radio warnings. It forced Doolittle to make a snap decision and launch the aircraft hours earlier than planned.

At 8am, still around 800 miles from Japan, the 16 bombers – each with a crew of five – successfully roared off the deck

A B-25B Mitchell bomber of the raid launches from the deck of *Hornet*. ✪

Lieutenant Robert L Hite was co-pilot of the 16th crew and was one of Americans to be captured by Chinese forces. He's pictured, blindfolded, being led from a Japanese transport plane after he and seven fellow raiders were flown from Shanghai to Tokyo to face trial. Hite was one of the four to remain imprisoned for the duration of the war, liberated more than three years later on August 20, 1945. ✪

of *Hornet* on their way to carry out what they knew would be a small, but they hoped would be a significant, strike against the heart of enemy territory. As well as generating much-needed natural resources, Japan's expansion had been based around creating an unbreakable barrier within which its home islands were untouchable. The Americans were sure that an early incursion, however minimal, would send ripples to the very top of Japan's proud and powerful high command.

Despite concerns that Japan had been alerted to their presence by the small skirmish en route to the launch point, Doolittle and his airmen encountered little in the way of resistance as each managed to reach the intended target. In total, the raid destroyed 112 buildings and killed 87 men, women and children. Owing to the nature of Japan's infrastructure, military installations, industrial areas and civilian dwellings were often close together – and more than 300 were reported as being injured.

While the damage inflicted was not on the same level as the Pearl Harbor attack or the Japanese conquests in Asia and the Pacific, the psychological impact was exactly as America had intended. In Tokyo, the Japanese released distorted figures and claimed that nine of the raiders had been shot down having only caused a

few minor fires. The reality was far more embarrassing, and military leaders were left scratching their heads as to how the US had managed to engineer and execute such a bold operation. One such person, the officer in charge of Tokyo's air defences, committed ritual suicide because of the supposed dishonour he had bought to himself by not being able to protect his country from American attack.

Among the Japanese population, and despite the government's attempts to play it down, the raid had created panic and confusion. The crews were flying at such low altitude over Tokyo that they had concerns about coming into contact with powerlines, and one crewmember later recalled how his aircraft had been close enough to the ground to interrupt a baseball game in the Tokyo suburbs. It was a sight which ignited great fear. The campaign had the desired effect in America, too, and when its events were officially announced by the US government a few weeks later, it gave the public a huge morale boost.

All 16 of the bomber crews made it out of Japan but the secret nature of the raid combined with the uncertain situation in China meant that the proposed airfields where the B-25Bs were supposed to land had never even been notified of the mission. As it turns out, it would have made little

difference because the early launch had left the aircraft short of fuel to make it to the intended destinations.

One pilot had jettisoned fuel in order to escape a Japanese fighter plane and so made the decision to fly northwest across Japan to Vladivostok in Russia; the crew landed safely but were interned by the officially neutral Russian authorities for 13 months before being secretly allowed out of the country through Iran.

The 15 others flew south through the Japanese islands before crossing the East China Sea to mainland Asia where the crews were forced to either crash-land or bail out along the Chinese coast – unaware of what was awaiting them on the ground. And indeed, what they encountered was a dire situation with many thousands of Japanese troops already in China, but not having established firm control of areas outside its major cities. Some crew were captured almost immediately, but some fell into the hands of friendly Chinese civilians who risked their lives to move the Americans from town to town and eventually to safety.

Of the eight men who were captured – all of them becoming prisoners of war – three were executed in October 1942 for crimes against Japanese civilians, another died while being held captive, with the other four

Yamamoto had predicted that if America could not be defeated early then Japan would have to face a powerful resurgence. In June, 1942, he was proved right as US forces won a stunning victory in the central Pacific...

The June 7 edition of the *Chicago Tribune* reports on the crucial developments. ✪

been secured, the process of extraction and transport alone meant it would be some months before these could fully bear fruit and at a time when measured reflection and consolidation was most required Japanese thinking was frenzied and reactionary.

In attempting to understand Japan's increasingly risky military strategy the psychological effect of the Doolittle Raid cannot be underestimated, particularly when considering the actions of Yamamoto who seemed to take the largely symbolic assault as a personal insult. It was surely impossible that America, the beleaguered nation that had offered little physical objection to the conquest of Allied territory, could mount such an operation with so little time to plan and prepare.

The anger he felt began to influence his actions, as did frustration and regret that his initial attempts to cement an early victory had failed. Japan could, and perhaps should, have defended what it had

gained; but with Yamamoto at the forefront of national military planning the dice was rolled on two hastily arranged operations that would aim to secure de facto control of Australia – albeit without actually entering the country – and extend its territory and influence to beyond halfway to the American west coast.

The campaign would begin with the successful invasion of key strategic locations in the Solomon Islands and New Guinea at the start of May, and would end with the glorious defeat of America's last remaining aircraft carriers deep into the Pacific Ocean by early June. Instead – in an eventful flurry of action that ended at Midway, the Combined Fleet was depleted, Japan's high command embarrassed and its population left facing economic turmoil and crippling material shortages.

America was buoyed, and set about the total destruction of its enemy with vigour. Japan, wanting to protect what it still had,

reverted to its traditional defensive posture and as it entered into a war of attrition it had little hope of sustaining was left to reflect on how and why it had all gone so horribly and drastically wrong.

Douglas TBD-1 Devastator aircraft, armed with torpedoes, prepare for launch on American carrier USS *Enterprise* during the critical Battle of Midway. ✪

CHAPTER 8

America cracks the code

In a cold and damp basement at Pearl Harbor, US intelligence officers were feverishly intercepting and analysing Japanese communications throughout the Pacific War. Their efforts would turn out to be one of America's most powerful tools...

In the report that followed the *Chicago Tribune's* emphatic headline announcing American victory at Midway was the suggestion that US forces had managed to acquire advance knowledge of Japanese movements in the Pacific. At the time such intelligence efforts were highly classified, and on August 7 the US government ordered an investigation into how exactly the *Tribune* had come to possess such facts. Part of the reason the story created such anxiety – aside from there being the potential for a dangerous leak within high-ranking military offices – was the fact that its contents were remarkably accurate, and indeed America had been able to predict where and when Japan planned to strike.

The encryption of sensitive messages and the deciphering of intercepted communications was one of the few areas of military operations in which the US had been well ahead of Japan in the build-up to the Second World War.

American code breakers had enjoyed a great deal of success in their efforts to unpick top-level Japanese naval codes since the 1920s, owing largely to the fact that Japan relied upon book-based ciphers rather than the more technologically advanced and harder to break mechanical equipment such as Germany's Enigma or Lorenz machines.

Captain Joseph J Rochefort – the man who handpicked and led many of the code breakers at Station HYPO. ✪

Japanese book ciphers

As the name suggests, a book cipher involves a code book where commonly used words and phrases are assigned a group of letters and numbers which becomes its code word. The book can either be a specially created code key, or any standard publication can be used as long as both ends of the message are in possession of the same 'key' text.

This allows the sender to compose a message, consult the chosen code book and encrypt those commonly used words and phrases, as well as changing any remaining text a character at a time. Once received, the same code book can be used to decipher the original meaning.

An added layer of encryption can be added by encoding the code book itself – this is called superenciphering.

A US naval radio station at Lualualei on Oahu, part of Station HYPO. ✪

Station HYPO: Learning from past mistakes

Known outside its own walls as the Combat Intelligence Unit, Station HYPO was one of three Pacific Fleet communications intelligence stations along with Station CAST in the Philippines and Station NEGAT at navy headquarters in Washington, DC. Before the outbreak of the Pacific War, the trio was responsible for decrypting Japanese radio traffic coming from both the home islands and its Pacific-based forces.

While the facility is thought of as one single location, it was actually a network of small offices and listening stations dotted across Oahu – but the bulk of the analytic work took place in the basement of an administrative building at Pearl Harbor known by its inhabitants as The Dungeon.

Joe Rochefort reported as officer in charge of Station HYPO on June 2, 1941, and immediately set about the challenging task of turning the high-grade work of this advanced unit into relevant operational intelligence. On his arrival he found that the information-gathering and cryptanalytic work taking place was bringing results, but the facility lacked the manpower to take

the raw data and provide the Pacific Fleet command with the required information.

He took a desk at the centre of The Dungeon, a journalist who later wrote a book on Rochefort describing it as similar to a city newspaper editor directing a newsroom full of "prima donnas, free spirits, grizzled veterans and eccentrics".

There were, however, many obstacles – and two main difficulties Rochefort faced was that he needed more bodies to churn through the data, and he needed more data to work with; because of Japan's efforts to maintain secrecy for the Pearl Harbor operation there was intended radio silence. With diplomacy failing at the end of the year and war becoming more and more of a possibility, HYPO made frantic efforts to unpick Japan's code and locate its sizeable fleets. However, because the task of decrypting messages was split between the three intelligence stations, key information was sometimes not being recognised and Rochefort pushed for his unit to assume full responsibility – he would eventually get his wish, but not before America suffered its crushing defeat at Pearl Harbor.

Understanding JN25

Without access to the code book, there was certainly no easy way to uncover an intercepted communication. However, America had devoted time and effort to developing its use of cryptanalysis and so had the resource to begin unlocking Japan's main naval cipher, dubbed JN25. It was a task that fell to the Fleet Radio Unit Pacific – also known as Station HYPO – a cryptanalytic department of the US Navy that was assigned responsibility to work on the systems of its Japanese counterparts with the renowned Captain Joseph J Rochefort at the helm.

While the group was developing some of the most advanced code-breaking techniques of the time, breaking book ciphers was as much about human analysis and pattern recognition as it was mathematics and technical applications. For the team based at an administration building in Pearl Harbor, uncovering Japanese communications was an exercise in puzzle-solving, understanding context and continual cross reference of communications to spot consistencies.

In the weeks and months after Pearl Harbor the frequency of Japanese messages was greatly increased owing to both its multitude of military operations and much wider geography. The increased chatter gave HYPO much more data to work with, and in early 1942 it had become increasingly confident in telegraphing Japan's next moves – declaring with a degree of certainty that another attack on America was in the offing and the target was encoded as AF. Simultaneously, radio signals were intercepted that indicated a Japanese offensive towards Australia and when the code RZP – already identified as Japan's designation for Port Moresby – was linked to talk of an invasion force, the Allies were able to get ahead of the game. The discovery that two major aircraft carriers were part of the force confirmed that the Coral Sea was the intended route for the invading party, and America was able to direct its own fleet to prevent the capture of the key New Guinean city.

Even after America managed to stop Japan's advance in the Coral Sea, AF was still being discussed by Japan – much to the concern of US military leaders. Rochefort believed the focus of the proposed campaign to be in the central Pacific region, and it was a theory supported by the fact that other communications had suggested the Japanese navy was preparing supplies for a long-distance strike. Could Japan be considering another attack on Hawaii? Was Midway a viable target? HYPO determined that Midway was in Japanese sights, and convinced Admiral Nimitz of its findings.

Washington was less certain, and navy officers there could not comprehend that Japan would send its mighty combined fleet for the sake of a small atoll; they had not understood just how incensed Yamamoto had been by the Doolittle Raid, and how convinced he had become that it had launched from Midway. The arguments went back and forth until a US naval intelligence officer at HYPO – Wilfred J Jasper Holmes – came up with a brilliant ruse to confirm finally whether or not the

Given the nature of the classified work taking place at HYPO, there are few pictures in existence from inside the America's Pacific code breaking hub. This one was taken in late 1945. ✪

Pacific territory was represented by AF.

Knowing that the island depended on desalinated water, he used an old undersea cable to send out a non-coded message pretending that the purification system had broken down, and stated: "We have only enough water for two weeks. Please supply us immediately." Just days later, HYPO picked up a communication from Japan detailing AF's water problems and that additional fresh water would be needed for its campaign; Rochefort's suspicions had been confirmed. In addition, US code breakers were able to determine that a small Japanese force would be sent further north to the Aleutian Islands as a diversion.

Unlike the surprise assault on Pearl Harbor, the Pacific Fleet was now armed with the knowledge of where and when Japan would hit next. Nimitz's confidence in HYPO's intelligence persuaded him to risk America's three remaining carriers to devise an ambush operation. The time had arrived to strike back, and Yamamoto steamed straight into the trap.

As Japanese planes swarmed across the skies, HYPO's team was underground in The Dungeon already attempting to understand how it had managed to overlook what was happening above. There have been many presentations on the mistakes America made that allowed such devastation to take place, but despite some of the operational missteps that had occurred at HYPO, perhaps the most telling reason why it was unable to give Pacific Fleet command any warning was what historian John Lundstrom aptly described as "a failure of imagination". At the heart of intelligence gathering is the process of human interpretation, and no one studying Japan's movements prior to 1941 imagined them capable of such an aggressive and audacious move. Rochefort, however, held himself to account and believed he had failed in his main purpose of providing operational intelligence to the US Navy's leaders. He vowed there would be no repeat.

There was understandable scepticism of HYPO in the days and weeks after Japan's Hawaiian raid, and Rochefort knew that establishing his unit's credibility was paramount. He had to provide evidence to Admiral King and Nimitz that he could give them the advantage by accurately predicting Japanese movements and, while it would take time, a series of small successes built trust and confidence. It reached a point where Nimitz was prepared to stake his Pacific Fleet on Rochefort's recommendations, and it was a decision that carried his forces to their game-changing victory at Midway.

THE DUNGEON
Nicknamed for its freezing temperatures, concrete floors and poor ventilation The Dungeon was at least spacious, if not comfortable. The office comprised four main sections, each carrying out a body of work required of America's top codebreaking team:

CRYPTANALYSIS:
Headed by Lieutenant Commander Thomas H Dyer, and assisted by fellow officers Ham Wright and Jack S Holtwick, this team conducted the difficult task of decrypting the plethroa of Japanese (and other) radio traffic into a useable form – and they did so with little more than pen and paper. The three excelled at mathematics.

TRAFFIC ANALYSIS:
Lieutenant Commanders Thomas A Huckins and John A Williams, plus two assistants, were more concerned with the intelligence surrounding intercepted messages than their content. The team studied patterns and uncovered relationships between the sender and receiver looking for clues as to the location and movement of Japanese forces. ✪

SHIP PLOTTING:
Lieutenant Jasper Holmes and his assistant Yeoman Willam Dunbar were not intelligence officers, but armed with little more than a table, Pacific Ocean charts and plotting equipment used the gathered intelligence to predict the movements, activity and intentions of vessels off America's west coast.

TRANSLATION:
Alva B Lasswell was a US Marine captain who had studied Japanese for three years in Tokyo as part of an exchange programme and later worked as a linguist in Shanghai. Initially part of a two-man team along with Lieutenant Ranson Fullwinder, the duo were joined in the autumn of 1941 by five further translators.

CHAPTER 9

The battle lines are drawn

As the dust settled on Japan's Pearl Harbor offensive and the opening moves in its campaign of expansion, it became clear that the Australian region was going to become a major battleground in the Pacific War...

As Japan swept south towards Australia and launched bombing raids on the northern city of Darwin, the threat of a Japanese invasion loomed large. The majority of Australia's own military forces – both in terms of equipment and personnel – had already been committed to the Mediterranean to support Britain's fight against Nazi Germany, so the government began overhauling economic and industrial policies to make Australia ready for total war. Given that the Pearl Harbor attack had now brought the US to the front and centre of conflict, Australian Prime Minister John Curtin also reached out to American leaders and called for a joint effort. It amounted to a plea for aid and Roosevelt paid heed.

With prosperous Asian territories now off-limits, Australia had come to the fore as one of America's biggest trading partners; and more pertinently to the war effort, it also had the potential to become the Allied stronghold in the region from which Japan's new-found supremacy could be challenged.

As the Japanese offensive began to run out of steam due to lack of resources and the sheer size of the territory it now had to defend, a full-scale invasion of Australia became a much less likely prospect. Roosevelt and Curtin took the opportunity to strengthen their ties as British authority in the region crumbled under the enormous pressure of its efforts to maintain a foothold in Europe. The American and British governments agreed that Australia would become a strategic responsibility of the US, and in March 1942 General Douglas MacArthur arrived to assume command of Australia's military units in the newly designated South West Pacific Area.

While the Americans accepted that it was simply impossible to defend Guam, Wake Island and the Philippines or assist Britain with the protection of other territories, and that losing control of those regions would be damaging but not disastrous, Australia was a different matter. If Japan was able to either invade or isolate Australia, it would be difficult for America

An Australian-produced propaganda poster released in 1942 warns of Japanese invasion. This artwork was criticised for being far too alarmist, and was banned by the Queensland state government. ✪

to ever re-establish itself in the Pacific. It was also supposed that if Yamamoto's Navy could swallow Australia into the Pacific defensive perimeter then perhaps Hawaii or even the US west coast would be next, particularly if Midway was captured.

Japan, likewise, realised that Australia was pivotal. With invasion ruled out, Admiral Inoue's plans to occupy Tulagi and Port Moresby – and later all of the Solomons, Fiji, Samoa and New Caledonia – were aimed at doing exactly what America feared; cutting off any supply lines from Australia to the US mainland across the Pacific Ocean.

The devastation of Pearl Harbor aside, the opening chapters of the Pacific War were largely concerned with the occupation of territory. The violent and bloody engagements being played out were about tactical positioning; putting the pieces on the board in place to enforce a victory, rather than being end goals in themselves. The nature of the game shifted when Japan targeted Australia, and it became apparent that this was the key region where the remainder of the Pacific War was going to be played out.

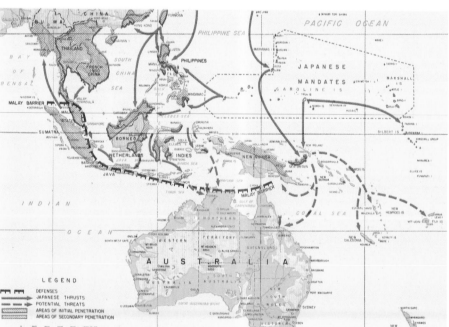

A map produced by the staff of General Douglas MacArthur that shows the actual Japanese advances during the first stages of the Pacific War, as well as the Empire's proposed targets. ✪

A reconnaissance photograph by a Royal Australian Air Force Hudson Mk IV taken on January 9 shows a concentration of enemy ships at Japan's Truk naval base ahead of the rumoured invasion. The operation to capture this image involved a return flight of 1405 miles which made it the longest sea reconnaissance that the RAAF had ever undertaken in a land-based aircraft. ✪

During the early months of the Pacific campaign, Australian troops attempted to hold areas of New Guinea virtually alone. Once the American war machine was in operation the two nations' forces were combined and here, in September 1942, soldiers of the Royal Australian Artillery man guns at Milne Bay airfield while a United States Kittyhawk prepares to land in the background. ✪

The battle for Port Moresby

There would have been few in the 1930s – as tensions increased between the US and Japan – who would have predicted the largest city on the island of New Guinea would become one of the key strategic pawns in a conflict between the two. Even fewer might have suggested that the contest between invasion and defence of Port Moresby would lead to a major confrontation between the nations' respective naval forces. However, with the location providing America with one of its last access routes into the South Pacific islands, and Japan realising the city's potential to become a base for a land-based bombers to target Australia, it became a must-hold for the US and a much sought-after acquisition for the Japanese.

Port Moresby was very much within reach, too. Japan already possessed a large and established facility at Truk in the

Caroline Islands lying directly between the Japanese mainland to the north and New Guinea to the south. It had become a Japanese colony during the First World War, and in the years after was turned into what was described as 'Japan's Pearl Harbor' – it being home to part of the combined Japanese fleet and giving berths to carriers such as *Akagi* and *Kaga*. Like Pearl Harbor, the aerial capabilities of Truk were substantial, with four separate airfields and storage for 77,200 tons of fuel oil – the

largest depot Japan possessed outside of the home islands.

Land-based aircraft at Truk were still not quite capable of reaching Australia; but their range was more than long enough to attack targets on the northern tips of New Guinea. Truk's proximity to the Australian territory was also ideal for carrier-based operations. On January 4, 1942, an invasion force departed Truk for Rabaul – a deep water harbour on the smaller island of New Britain – while carrier attack groups

Senior Allied commanders are pictured at Port Moresby, October 1942. From left to right: Frank Forde, Australian Minister for the Army; General Douglas MacArthur; Allied forces Supreme Commander South West Pacific Area; Sir Thomas Blamey, Allied Land Forces; Lieutenant General George C Kenny, Allied Air Forces; Lieutenant General Edmund Herring, New Guinea Force; Brigadier General Kenneth Walker, V Bomber Command, Fifth Air Force.

John Curtin, Australian Prime Minister from 1941-1945. He was a strong advocate of much closer bonds with the US in the face of Japanese aggression. ✪

Australian forces retreat from Rabaul across the Warangoi river in January 1942. Blistering Japanese air attacks had pushed the limited Australian defences back into these sorts of unfavourable positions, and it would not take long for Imperial Army troops to begin campaigns against the defenders. ✪

launched ferocious air raids in large numbers to soften up Australian defences. Given that the defence consisted of little more than 2000 men – only 700 of whom were trained soldiers – the 5000-strong invasion force would probably have been able to succeed alone.

The air attacks had done their job though, and by the time Japanese troops entered the region on January 23 there were only small pockets of Australian resistance that had spread to positions away from the main harbour area. Occupiers soon got to work and a major naval base quickly developed, along with an army barracks and other support structures. At its peak in 1943, there were around 110,000 Japanese troops stationed at Rabaul.

With a position established on New Guinea's smaller outlying lands, the focus turned to Port Moresby. Japan had edged closer to Australia, but still couldn't threaten its major cities with land-based bombers, and so the Guinean harbour seemed like the perfect location to target. At the time there was no major American military presence there, and given its earlier successes in wrestling control of territory from the US, Japanese commanders foresaw little difficulty in the operation. They had made invasion plans by early May. Unbeknownst to them however, American code breakers had uncovered the plot and the Pacific Fleet was able to successfully fend off the advance in what became the Battle of the Coral Sea.

The Royal Australian Navy heavy cruiser HMAS *Canberra* is under way off Tulagi during Allied landings there in August 1942. The campaign was part of the first phase of the America-led fightback in the South West Pacific Area. ✪

For Japan, however, Port Moresby was the key to subduing growing American power and strength in Australia and, despite the initial setback, it would not be deterred. If the city couldn't be taken from the sea Japan would reach it by land and, with its troops having already set foot on terra firma in the north of New Guinea in March, plans were drawn up to move these forces south through the jungles and invade Port Moresby that way.

Of further concern for the Allied nations was the discovery that the Imperial Navy had secretly begun construction of a large airfield at Lunga Point on nearby Guadalcanal in the Solomon Islands – also close enough for land-based bombers to theoretically strike Australia.

It had always been the intention of US command – directed by Roosevelt himself – that when the time was right America would begin a measured push back against the Japanese, taking one village at a time if had to. That time, it seemed, had arrived. As early as March, Admiral King had advocated the Solomon Islands as the starting point for the first major Allied land offensive of the conflict, and after Japan's sensational defeat at Midway the plans were escalated. Pivotal naval skirmishes would make the headlines for much of mid-1942, but during this same period the action taking place across the Australian region was laying the foundations for an all-encompassing American war effort that was to come.

MacArthur (left) and Curtin developed a close relationship during the American general's time in Australia as head of the Allied South West Pacific forces, and the pair are shown here in conversation. ✪

From Coral Sea to Midway:
America turns the tide

Japan enjoyed total domination for the first six months of the
Pacific War, but the time had come for America to make a stand.
The two defining naval battles of the conflict were about to begin...

Despite heavy anti-aircraft fire, Japanese
torpedo bombers manage to land strikes
on carrier USS *Yorktown*. While *Yorktown*
would eventually go under as a result of the
damage sustained, there were far graver
consequences for the Japanese fleet. ✪

By the end of April 1942 the scene had been set for one of the Pacific War's most intense periods of action. Finally, after months of retreating and consolidating rather than risking its forces in defence of the Philippines and other Asia-Pacific territories, America declared 'no more'. With key intelligence information on the whereabouts and intentions of the Imperial Japanese Navy in hand, the US leadership decided the time had come to confront the enemy and committed its Pacific Fleet carriers first to prevent a Japanese invasion of Port Moresby in New Guinea, north of Australia, and then to counter a strike on Midway Island.

The first engagement at Coral Sea was by no means an outright victory for the US, and it was America that suffered the heaviest losses when its carrier USS *Lexington* had to be scuttled following a savage Japanese air attack. In comparison, Japan's only fatality was light carrier *Shoho* – but crucially two of its main fleet carriers also suffered significant damage and it was enough for the occupation of Port Moresby to be abandoned by the Imperial Navy. The US claimed a tactical victory.

Perhaps the biggest impact of the Battle of the Coral Sea, however, was that Japan's two damaged carriers – *Shokaku* and *Zuikaku* – were part of the mighty

Combined Fleet and as a result of the wounds sustained were forced to withdraw from Yamamoto's Midway incursion. It ensured that when the group set sail for the central Pacific there was now a numerical parity between the Japanese and American carrier air units.

That parity, combined with the United States' successful efforts to predict Japanese tactics and ambush its fleet ahead of invasion, led to what was described by British military historian John Keegan as "the most stunning and decisive blow in the history of naval warfare". Under the command of Admirals Chester Nimitz, Frank Fletcher and Raymond Spruance, the crucial element of surprise was utilised to devastating effect as the less experienced forces of the Pacific Fleet created a state of chaos and confusion among the Japanese ranks and obliterated its four-strong carrier group along with several escort ships.

At Coral Sea, Japan enjoyed the relative luxury of being able to recall its invasion force without great losses; at Midway the US gave Yamamoto no such option and the shell-shocked Japanese admiral, with no air cover, was forced to halt the entire operation after just two days of action. Port Moresby had slipped through Japan's grasp, and any chance it had of occupying Midway had been ripped out of its hands

by the US assault. While the Imperial Navy had successfully wrestled control of Tulagi and the Aleutian Islands from its now-confident and vengeful enemy, rather than beginning the summer of 1942 with strategic dominance in the Pacific region it faced the prospect of having to defend prone territory without being able to call on its mighty aircraft carriers for support.

Proud and determined, Japan would dig in and fight with every means at its disposal as victory slipped further and further out of its grasp. Try as it might, however, the country simply couldn't escape the impact of its debilitating defeat at Midway and amidst economic strife and muddled tactical thinking would slip further and further behind the US in nearly every aspect.

In the immediate aftermath of the battle, across the Pacific to the west, triumphant American officers began compiling official accounts of what had occurred. The following pages are a presentation of those combat narratives published by the United States Navy Office of Naval Intelligence, furnished with other detail that has since been uncovered or revealed as a result of study or declassification. Together, they tell the story of a five-week turning point in history that ended with America beginning what became an unstoppable march towards total victory in the Pacific Theatre.

A crewmember of a Douglas TBD-1 torpedo bomber captures USS *Yorktown* operating in the Pacific shortly after taking off from the carrier's deck, while other aircraft prepare for launch. This photograph was taken in February 1942 as the US carriers attempted but failed to thwart Japan's initial invasion operations. They would be much more successful in later weeks and months as they used American intelligence gathering to track and counter Japanese Navy movements. ✪

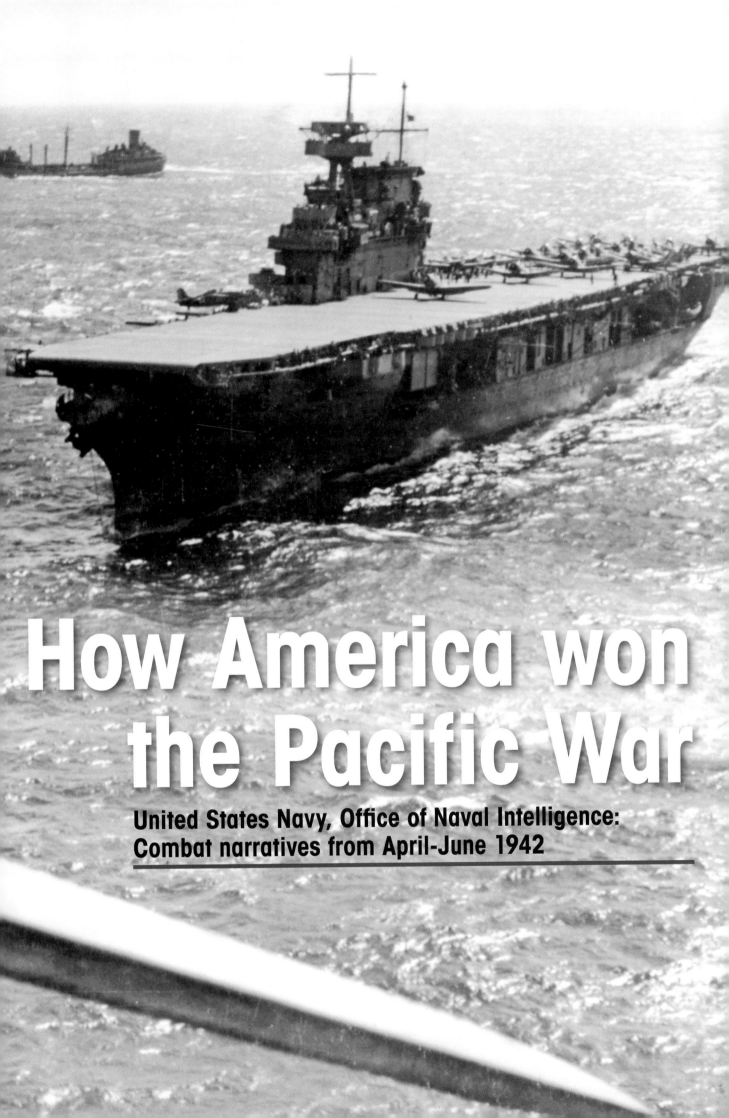

How America won the Pacific War

United States Navy, Office of Naval Intelligence:
Combat narratives from April-June 1942

APRIL 15 |

As it becomes clear defending the northern coast of Australia will be vital to American interests, USS *Lexington* arrives in the South Pacific to bolster US strength in the region.

APRIL 18 |

James Doolittle leads 16 B-25B bombers off the deck of USS *Hornet* to strike at targets on the Japanese home islands. It would be America's first 'victory' of the conflict.

APRIL 21 |

Joseph Rochefort's team at Pearl Harbor's Station HYPO intercepts a Japanese radio message noting carriers *Shokaku* and *Zuikaku* are being detached to the South Pacific.

APRIL 21 |

A large number of Japanese warships are dispatched to search for the carriers that launched the Doolittle Raid.

APRIL 22 |

HYPO correctly places Japanese carriers *Shokaku*, *Zuikaku* and light carrier *Shoho* at the Japanese base in Rabaul, along with a large concentration of other warships – but also mistakenly suggests that *Kaga* is present.

APRIL 24 |

Japanese Navy radio messages reveal the existence of task forces with names such as MO Covering Force, MO Attack Force and RZP Occupation Force. Rochefort quickly communicates that these groups are intended for an attack against Port Moresby.

APRIL 27 |

Rochefort's team reports that the Imperial Japanese Navy has changed the call signs of its major warships, a potential indicator of a major military operation.

APRIL 29 |

Japan's Special Naval Landing Force departs Rabaul in preparation for the invasion of the Australian seaplane base at Tulagi. Meanwhile, further transports load equipment necessary for building new facilities at Port Moresby. Back in Hawaii, Rochefort's unit decode parts of a message from Admiral Yamamoto to Admiral Inoue in which northern Australia is mentioned; giving credence to theories that Port Moresby is under threat.

APRIL 30 |

Such is Rochefort's confidence that the Guinean city is a target, he sends a report to Admiral Nimitz. It's clear that the operation has multiple objectives, and Rochefort advises that HYPO intelligence also points to an additional attack on Tulagi.

MAY 1

Japan's Port Moresby invasion force departs Rabaul, escorted by seven cruisers and one light carrier, on the same day that three US B-26 Marauder bombers strike Rabaul causing damage to an aircraft. In preparation for the Tulagi invasion, Japanese forces bomb the Solomon Islands destroying an Australian PBY Catalina aircraft. Further afield, *Lexington* and USS *Yorktown* rendezvous east of Australia near the New Hebrides. Back at Pearl Harbor, intelligence gathering is now a 24-hour-a-day operation and Rochefort reports that Port Moresby is still the likely target of an attack, the Australian mainland is not under threat for now and Japanese reconnaissance operations are increasing east in the Pacific and near the Aleutian Islands.

MAY 2

Nimitz has already made the decision to allow the invasion of Tulagi in order to concentrate his forces on defending Port Moresby. Another Japanese aerial attack against the Tulagi seaplane base signals the imminent arrival of hostile troops and Australian personnel are evacuated. Allied spotters across Guinea and the Solomon Islands report that a large force of Japanese ships is on the move.

MAY 3

Naval troops from Japan's Kure Special Landing Force arrive at Tulagi and swiftly seize the territory. The invasion party quickly gets to work on installing a communications network. While the US was unable to counter the ground offensive, a day before she was scheduled to regroup with *Lexington* in the Coral Sea, *Yorktown* gets into position to launch air raids against the unsuspecting Japanese Navy in the harbour at Tulagi.

MAY 4

07.01: *Yorktown* launches her first strike wave consisting of 12 TBD Devastator torpedo bombers and 28 SBD Dauntless dive bombers.

08.50: The force takes Japanese ships by surprise at anchor and causes major damage to the destroyer *Kikuzuki* before inflicting minor wounds on minelayer *Okinoshima*. The remaining ships begin escaping the harbour, fearing further attacks.

12.10: A second wave from *Yorktown* arrives and targets ships which are now steaming away from the harbour at full speed; two minesweepers are sunk and another severely damaged. Four F4F-3/3A Wildcat fighters are launched to defend the bombers, but they also strafe the destroyer *Yuzuki*, killing her captain and nine other crewmen.

15.30: A smaller third wave causes further damage to a Japanese freighter. Later in the evening, *Yorktown* moves from her position near Guadalcanal and heads south-east to join up with *Lexington*.

1. Armed aircraft aboard the advancing Japanese fleet carrier *Zuikaku* are pictured on May 5. The vessel is east of the Solomon Islands and advancing on Guinea's Port Moresby to provide aerial support for the Imperial Navy's invasion operation. ✪
2. A wave breaks on the deck of USS *Neosho* while she refuels USS *Yorktown* at sea on May 1. ✪
3. A view of the seaplane base on Tulagi. This image was actually taken by the crew of an SBD-3 bomber from USS *Saratoga* during a later American operation in the Solomon Islands. ✪
4. A Douglas TBD-1 Devastator of Torpedo Squadron Five which operated from *Yorktown* during the Tulagi air raids. ✪
5. The rusting hull of Japanese destroyer *Kikuzuki* photographed in Tulagi in August 1943 after US forces had dragged the wreckage onto the beach. ✪
6. USS *Lexington* is seen from the deck of *Yorktown* after the two had rendezvoused in the Coral Sea to confront the advancing Japanese fleet. ✪
7. Douglas SBDs of *Yorktown* head back to the carrier after a strike on Japanese ships in Tulagi harbour. ✪

1

MAY 4 |

2

Allied planes take off from Queensland and Horn Island in Australia, as well as from Port Moresby itself, to search for the Japanese task force at sea. A B-25 bomber spots light carrier *Shoho* and her group.

MAY 5 |

Shoho is sighted once more during the day, and so at night B-17 Flying Fortress bombers are armed and readied for a morning raid against the Japanese vessel.

MAY 6 |

Beginning in the early hours, the bombers depart from Port Moresby and arrive at *Shoho's* location shortly after 8am to begin their attack – but no damage is reported. The two US carriers *Yorktown* and *Lexington* meet with Australian cruisers to set up an ambush in the Coral Sea's Jomard Passage. As night draws in the American and Japanese fleets each launch aircraft in a bid to locate their opponents, but despite them being just 80 miles apart these attempts are unsuccessful. Back at Tulagi, defying US air raids, the Japanese seaplane base is now operational.

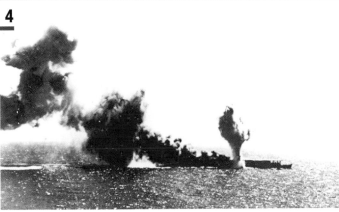

3

MAY 7 |

06.25: US Admiral Frank Fletcher, commanding the Coral Sea task force, sends the Australian cruiser group to prevent Japanese ships from slipping through the Jomard Passage while *Yorktown* and *Lexington* remain in position to seek and engage enemy ships. The separation weakens both units, but Fletcher deems it a necessary risk to prevent the invasion group reaching Port Moresby undetected. Aircraft from both sides spend the next hour frantically trying to locate each other.

07.22: A scout plane from Japan's carrier task force reports that it has located American ships and describes its findings as "one carrier, one cruiser and three destroyers", however the *Shokaku* aircraft had actually discovered and misidentified fleet oiler USS *Neosho* and destroyer USS *Sims*.

08.00: Vice Admiral Chuichi Hara – in tactical command – launches all of his available planes from *Shokaku* and *Zuikaku* towards the reported position. The force consists of 18 Zero fighters, 36 D3A dive-bombers and 24 torpedo-armed bombers.

08.15: An SDB from *Yorktown* sights vessels protecting the Port Moresby invasion convoy, but an error in a coded message means a report is mistakenly received stating the pilot has seen two Japanese carriers. As a result, Fletcher orders all available carrier aircraft – 18 Wildcats, 53 Dauntless and 22 Devastators – to the attack. The message was meant to read "two cruisers and four destroyers", but that was also incorrect as the group the pilot had spotted included *Shoho*.

1. The wing of a Val dive-bomber blends into the Coral Sea below as its crew captures the Japanese air attack in pursuit of American ships. ✪
2. Fleet oiler USS *Neosho* in flames and sinking. ✪
3. Japanese light carrier *Shoho* shows clear signs of damage after coming under attack from US bombers, still visible above. ✪
4. Smoke continues to pour from the stricken light carrier. ✪
5. Further attacks begin to take their toll on *Shokaku* and signs of damage begin to show. ✪

1. A B5N2 bomber, equipped with torpedoes, launches from the deck of *Zuikaku*. ✪
2. A B5N Kate bomber having been hit by US anti-aircraft fire. ✪
3. USS *Lexington* steaming across the Coral Sea as its aircraft search for Japanese ships on the morning of May 8. ✪
4. Indicated by the stripe underneath its tail code, this D3A1 dive bomber launching from *Zuikaku* is most likely a command aircraft. ✪

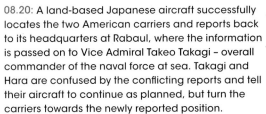

08.20: A land-based Japanese aircraft successfully locates the two American carriers and reports back to its headquarters at Rabaul, where the information is passed on to Vice Admiral Takeo Takagi – overall commander of the naval force at sea. Takagi and Hara are confused by the conflicting reports and tell their aircraft to continue as planned, but turn the carriers towards the newly reported position.

09.15: Japan's carrier aircraft reach *Neosho* and *Sims*, and begin searching for the American carriers that have been incorrectly placed nearby.

10.12: A trio of US B-17 bombers report having seen one carrier, 10 transports and 16 warships – the Port Moresby invasion force – 35 miles south of the location of its first sighting. Unsure if the two are related to the same group or not, Fletcher directs his already airborne attack towards the B-17's updated target area.

10.40: American strike aircraft reach *Shoho* and begin their attack runs. The light carrier is protected by only seven Japanese fighters with the rest of the aircraft being prepared below deck to launch against US ships. Cruisers attempt to defend *Shoho* with anti-aircraft fire, but *Lexington's* air group hits her with two bombs and five torpedoes scoring significant damage that starts rampant fires.

10.51: After more than an hour, *Shokaku* scouting crews realise their error, and it becomes clear the US carriers are now between the carriers and the invasion force, placing it under threat. He orders an immediate attack on *Neosho* and *Sims*, and then orders his aircraft to return to their carriers.

11.00: Back in the skies over *Shoho*, *Yorktown's* aircraft descend on the stationary vessel, landing at least 11 more bomb hits and two torpedo strikes.

11.15: To the south, Japan's airborne fighters and torpedo bombers abandon raids on *Neosho* and *Sims*, leaving the 36 dive bombers to wreak havoc. *Sims* is hit by three bombs, shatters in half and sinks immediately taking 178 of her 192-man crew down with her. *Neosho* suffers seven strikes, and to compound matters one of the dive bombers, hit by anti-aircraft fire, smashes into her. She's left drifting, slowly sinking and without power.

11.35: *Shoho*, having been ripped apart by the ferocious US air attack, sinks and the defending warships retreat to the north. A destroyer is sent back to rescue survivors, picking up just 203 of *Shoho's* 834-strong crew.

14.20: American aircraft have returned to their carriers, and are now rearmed and ready to launch against the Japanese invasion force or its warships. However both sides embark on a period of consolidation during which they are once again unable to pinpoint the enemy's location.

18.30: Confusion reigns as darkness falls. Several returning Japanese dive bombers find the American carriers and, thinking they are Japanese, prepare to land before being driven away by anti-aircraft fire. With nightfall ending operations for the day, the planned Port Moresby invasion is delayed until May 12 and Takagi is ordered to find and destroy *Lexington* and *Yorktown* the following day.

06.15: Hara launches aircraft to restart the search for the American carriers. Low-lying cloud that had obscured the US vessels the previous day is now covering the Japanese fleet with visibility as limited as just two miles.

06.35: 18 SBDs take off from American carriers to conduct a 360° search.

08.20: A *Lexington* SBD spies the Japanese carriers through a hole in the cloud cover and notifies the US task force.

08.22: Almost simultaneously, a search aircraft from *Shokaku* sights the American group, with the two fleets now about 240 miles apart.

09.15: In a flurry of action, both sides rush to launch their respective strike groups. Japan's flying force comprising 18 fighters, 33 dive bombers and 18 torpedo planes takes off. Six fighters, 24 dive bombers and nine torpedo planes are launched by *Yorktown*.

09.25: *Lexington's* force of nine fighters, 15 dive bombers and 12 torpedo planes go into action before both Japanese and American ships turn and head towards each other to shorten the distances planes will need to travel on their return legs.

10.55: Inbound Japanese aircraft are detected by *Lexington's* radar system and nine Wildcat fighters are sent to intercept, but six of them fly too low and miss the incoming attack group. The remaining trio do engage and an aerial dogfight ensues with four Japanese planes shot down. The remaining units descend and prepare to fire.

10.57: *Yorktown's* dive bombers locate the Japanese carriers, but wait for the slower torpedo planes to catch up in order to launch a simultaneous assault. *Shokaku* and *Zuikaku* are around 9000m apart, but low rain clouds over the latter make *Shokaku* the clearer target and the dive bombers begin their runs, hitting her with two 1000lb payloads. The damage to her flight deck and hangars is substantial. None of the torpedo aircraft are able to score a hit.

11.13: The US carriers are separated by just 2700m as their escort ships open fire on the advancing Japanese planes. Four torpedo bombers targeting *Yorktown* miss their mark.

11.20: *Lexington* is less fortunate, and suffers two hits. The first damages aircraft fuel tanks and releases flammable vapours into surrounding compartments. The second ruptures a water main and reduces the ship's power, although she's able to make 24 knots.

11.27: The 33 Japanese dive bombers descend from 14,000ft and hit *Lexington* twice, causing more damage and starting fires. *Yorktown* suffers severe structural damage too, as a single armour-piercing bomb penetrates four decks before exploding.

3

4

5

1. American aircraft manage to find *Shokaku* – making a sharp right turn – under heavy cloud cover, but the planes initially miss their target as evidenced by the eruptions of water. ✪
2. Fires rage aboard USS *Lexington* during the afternoon of May 8. An aircraft is just visible off her bow, most likely attempting to land on the US carrier. ✪
3. Flak bursts streak across the sky towards a burning *Lexington*. ✪
4. Debris is strewn among damaged aircraft on the deck of *Lexington*. ✪
5. Crew inspect the damage caused by a Japanese bomb on *Lexington's* number four gun. The crew manning it during the battle had been wiped out by the resulting explosion. ✪

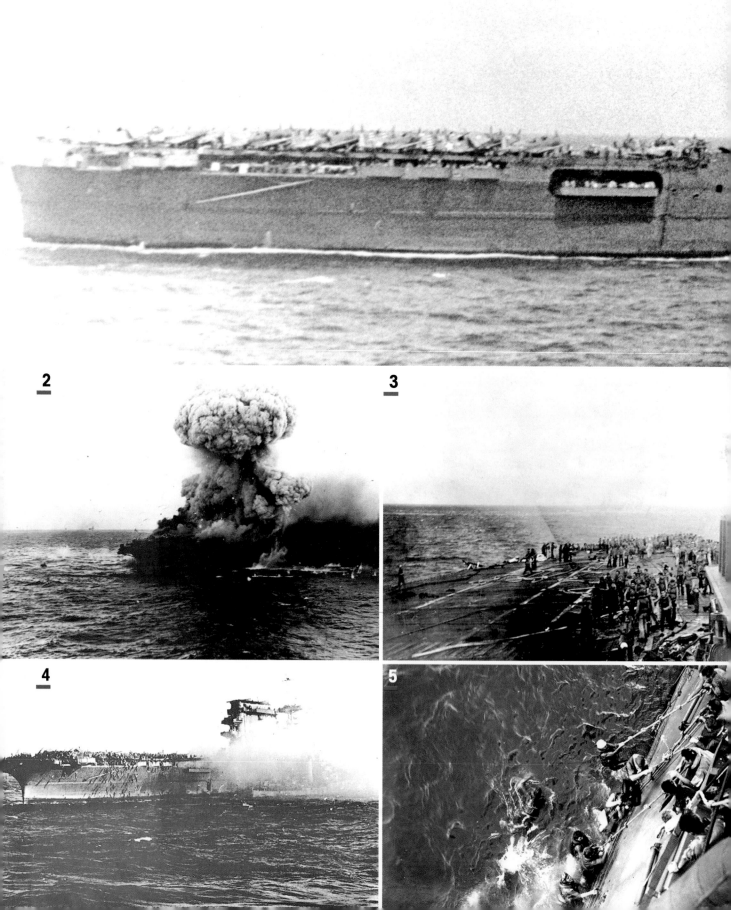

1. The last known picture of an operational USS *Lexington*. Taken from heavy cruiser USS *Portland*, the shot shows the carrier after initial damage control measures had been taken but before the large explosions and subsequent fires that would lead to her downfall. ✪
2. A photographer captures the moment *Lexington* is rocked by a huge explosion. ✪
3. Crew gather on *Lexington's* flight deck in preparation to abandon ship. ✪
4. The end is near for *Lexington* as its crews depart the stricken vessel. ✪
5. Survivors from *Lexington* are pulled aboard cruiser USS *Minneapolis*. ✪
6. Back in Japan, a photographer surveys bomb damage to the upper boat deck of *Shokaku*. ✪
7. Engineers work to repair the damaged *Shokaku*. The carrier was due to play a vital part in ongoing Pacific operations. ✪
8. A view from the underside of *Yorktown's* flight deck structure. The gaping hole was caused by a Japanese armour-piercing bomb which killed or seriously injured 66 crew when it ripped through four levels of the ship before exploding. ✪

Allied Blockade

A propaganda cartoon in the English-language Japanese publication, *Japan Times & Advertiser*, published on May 13, 1942. It depicts the Battle of the Coral Sea and shows a mournful Uncle Sam joining British leader Winston Churchill as they mark the graves of ships the Imperial Japanese Navy claim to have sunk up to this point of the Pacific War. While the references to the British ships are accurate, the Japanese declare they have sunk USS *Saratoga* and USS *Yorktown*, but in fact had destroyed USS *Lexington* and damaged *Yorktown*. Battleship USS *California* had been neutralised during the Pearl Harbor attack, but would return to service later in the conflict. ✪

11.30: The aerial bombardment of the Japanese fleet continues as *Lexington's* force arrives – a dive bomber scoring a hit with another 1000lb weapon causing further damage and intensifying fires which have broken out. The weather is kinder to and she *Zuikaku* continues to escape punishment.

12:00: By midday both air forces are on their way back to their fleets, with the Japanese pilots believing they'd inflicted fatal damage on two American carriers: *Yorktown* and *Lexington*. The aerial armadas pass each other en route and engage in further aircraft-to-aircraft altercations.

12.10: *Shokaku* has suffered extensive damage and 223 of her crew have been killed or wounded. She's unable to launch any further aircraft and requests to be withdrawn. Accompanied by two destroyers, she immediately retires to the north-east.

12.47: Crews work vigorously aboard *Lexington* to extinguish fires, but sparks from an unattended motor ignite the leaking aviation fuel fumes. The resulting explosion rocks the vessel and kills 25 men.

14.30: Early in the afternoon, the two carrier fleets have recovered aircraft from their returning attack groups, and begin to count the cost of what was to become known as the Battle of the Coral Sea – the first major naval engagement where the opposing ships never once sighted each other. Fletcher reports that both his carriers are damaged and his air groups have lost a significant number of Wildcat fighters. When pilots report that only one of the Japanese carriers was hurt, he withdraws and suggests the convoy is pursued by land-based bombers.

15.00: Takagi is notified that Japanese aircraft have 'sunk' two American carriers, but heavy aircraft losses and the departure of *Shokaku* means further operations are impossible. Inoue accepts the recommendation and recalls the Port Moresby invasion convoy – which has simultaneously been attacked by Australian groups – to Rabaul. He redirects his forces to begin the operation to capture Nauru and Ocean Island. The decision to postpone the Rabaul advance means Allied countries have successfully defended a Japanese invasion effort for the first time in the Pacific War.

15.25: Having already been stunned by a second explosion, a third blast starts multiple fires on *Lexington*, and the crew reports that the flames are out of control.

17.07: Having spent more than five hours trying to fight fires, *Lexington's* crew begin abandoning the vessel.

19.15: *Lexington's* survivors are rescued; the destroyer USS *Phelps* subsequently scuttles the burning ship by firing five torpedoes into her. Of the *Lexington's* 2951-man crew, 216 have been lost in the fighting.

MAY 9 |

As the inquest into events at the Coral Sea begins, Japanese carrier *Zuikaku* is ordered to pursue any American ships that remain in the region. Meanwhile, the injured *Shokaku* attempts to steam back to the home islands while avoiding US submarines which have been alerted to her journey. Back at Pearl Harbor, Station HYPO intelligence officers report an increasing level of activity by Yamamoto's Combined Fleet.

MAY 10 |

Japan's Operation RY invasion force, targeting Nauru and Ocean Island, departs Rabaul.

MAY 11 |

04.52: The Operation RY fleet consisting of two troopships, two destroyers, a cruiser and two minelayers sets sail from Rabaul – but the group is attacked by a US submarine causing damage to minelayer *Okinoshima*, forcing her to return to the base. The other escorts fight back, damage the American vessel, and continue. However, carriers USS *Enterprise* and *Hornet* act on intelligence about the proposed occupation and steam towards the area as a deterrent. It works, and fearing the threat posed by the American carriers and their aircraft the RY invasion convoy retreats to Rabaul.

13.00: American and Australian aircraft locate *Neosho* which has been adrift for four days and pick up survivors. In Hawaii, Rochefort – working around the clock to decipher Japanese naval communication – identifies that an occupation force is proceeding to the Marianas Islands. It emphasises his belief that Midway is the likely target.

MAY 12 |

Shokaku manages to avoid US submarines on her voyage home, but she's suffered extensive damage and nearly capsizes during the journey. In America, US Navy leaders in Washington, DC disagree with Rochefort's theory that Midway is under threat.

3

4

5

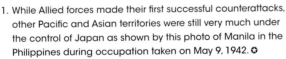

1. While Allied forces made their first successful counterattacks, other Pacific and Asian territories were still very much under the control of Japan as shown by this photo of Manila in the Philippines during occupation taken on May 9, 1942. ✪

2. At Pearl Harbor, Admiral Chester Nimitz presents awards to crew for their actions during the Japanese attack. The honours were bestowed at the end of May, and many of these men would soon be back in action on board ships headed for Midway. Capsized USS *Oklahoma* and sunken USS *West Virginia* and USS *Arizona* are visible in the background. ✪

3. USS *Enterprise* enters Pearl Harbor having been recalled from its South Pacific operations ahead of what seemed like inevitable action in the Central Pacific Ocean. ✪

4. A photograph from Pearl Harbor Naval Station shows aircraft carrier USS *Hornet* ahead of preparations for its journey to Midway Island. ✪

5. Kittyhawk fighters of the American Volunteer Group flying above the Salween River Gorge on the Chinese-Burmese border on May 28. The US forces are just trying to maintain the fight in Asia, while the country looks to make a decisive move toward victory by ambushing the Japanese fleet in the Pacific. ✪

MAY 13 |

HYPO officers continue to inform the Pacific Fleet of Japanese movements and plans; two messages are intercepted that request navigational charts of Oahu and instruct Japan's occupation force to pick up a seaplane unit. Rochefort determines that AF – the operation's destination – must either have or be capable of housing a seaplane base which only deepens his confidence in his Midway theory. Nimitz is yet to be fully convinced, and warns King that Hawaii or even the US west coast could be targets. In Japan, Yamamoto is granted a personal audience with Emperor Hirohito who congratulates him on the sinking of American carriers at Coral Sea. Knowing that actually the US had probably won the tactical battle by preventing the planned invasion of Port Moresby, Yamamoto is reluctant to accept the praise.

MAY 14 |

Rochefort presents his Midway analysis to Nimitz's war plans officer Lynde McCormick. Having forged a strong relationship with HYPO and having great confidence in its abilities, McCormick endeavours to convince Nimitz of the accuracy of Rochefort's findings.

MAY 15 |

Nimitz moves his two carriers – *Enterprise* and *Hornet* – from the South to central Pacific region although his superior King is still not sold on the idea of a Midway effort by the Japanese. Nimitz responds by stating his belief, supported by HYPO's intelligence, that Japan will attack Midway, the Aleutian Islands and Port Moresby in a trio of operations across a period of three weeks.

MAY 17 |

Repairs on *Shokaku* begin in Japan and she's placed in the Reserve Unit of the Mobile Force.

MAY 19 |

Lieutenant Commander Jasper Holmes devises a ruse to establish whether or not AF refers to Midway. His plan is to send out a fabricated message that the island's water distiller has broken down and the base desperately needs fresh supplies. At this time HYPO begins to pick up the mention of a new code name, MI, and determines that this is the operational name for the strike while AF definitely refers to the target.

MAY 20

With Japan having intercepted the fake communication, HYPO picks up an order to the Japanese invasion fleet to take additional supplies of fresh water. Holmes's scheme has worked, and the US now knows Midway is the target. US Navy and Marine forces are dispatched, and its carriers are instructed to maintain radio silence to avoid alerting the Japanese fleet.

MAY 24

All American warships in the Coral Sea are recalled to Pearl Harbor to prepare for countering Japan's attack.

MAY 27

From its rendezvous point in the Marianas Islands, an invasion fleet carrying 5000 Japanese troops departs for Midway. Naval and encryption codes for all Japanese fleets and bases are changed. *Yorktown* arrives at Pearl Harbor and 1400 maintenance workers are immediately directed to make necessary repairs in time for the defence of Midway.

MAY 28

USS *Tangier*, a seaplane tender, conducts a small raid on Tulagi. During the attack radio messages are transmitted intending to dupe the Japanese into believing the bombings have been carried out by a US aircraft carrier, and that its carrier fleet is still in the area and not at Pearl Harbor readying to counter Operation MI. *Hornet* and *Enterprise* both depart Hawaii on that day, to take a position off Midway.

MAY 29

After undergoing work in dry dock, *Yorktown* is re-floated, refuelled and readied for action before departing for Midway the next day.

MAY 30

The transport fleet of Japan's Aleutian invasion campaign sails out into the northern Pacific Ocean.

MAY 31

HYPO intercepts a Japanese message noting that *Zuikaku's* air group is being transferred, suggesting she will not be part of the Midway campaign. Indeed, the losses suffered by *Zuikaku's* aerial strike force during the Battle of Coral Sea mean she is unable to participate – and repairs to *Shokaku* will not be made in time. US intelligence accurately predicts that four Japanese carriers will be utilised – *Akagi*, *Kaga*, *Soryu* and *Hiryu*.

1. A B-17E Flying Fortress bomber of the US Army Air Force takes off from the air strip on Midway's Eastern Island on the afternoon of May 31. Knowing that a Japanese attack was imminent, aircraft were making regular patrols on a radius from the tiny Pacific atoll. ✪

2. Crew work on a Wildcat fighter at Oahu's Kaneohe Naval Station. The aircraft is set to take part in the Midway operation aboard a US aircraft carrier. ✪

3. An SB2U-3 Vindicator of the US Marine Corps takes off from Midway Island as plans are made to prepare the region for Japanese invasion. ✪

4. USS Yorktown steams into Pearl Harbor having made her way back from the Battle of the Coral Sea for repairs. ✪

5. F4F-3 Wildcats prepare to launch from USS Enterprise on May 12. The carrier had initially been dispatched towards the Coral Sea but arrived too late to take part in the battle. She was subsequently sent to deter Japan's Nauru and Ocean Island invasion campaign. ✪

5

JUNE 1 |

1

HYPO reports that Japan is monitoring carrier radio traffic in and around the Hawaiian islands, but Nimitz continues to position his fleet in defence of Midway. While it will take several days for her to arrive, USS *Saratoga* departs San Diego en route to Pearl Harbor in the hope that she can provide a late boost to the operation to defend Midway Island.

JUNE 2 |

Yorktown, Enterprise and *Hornet* rendezvous at a position 350 miles north-east of Midway, with Fletcher taking overall tactical command of the fleet. In addition, 25 US Navy submarines are deployed west of Midway in an attempt to detect the approach of the Japanese fleet.

JUNE 3 |

As confrontation at Midway looms on the horizon, US PBY Catalina aircraft discover the location of Japanese invasion transports west of the atoll. Nine land-based bombers are sent to attack and reach their targets at 6.30pm inflicting little damage. A group of Japanese submarines form a cordon from Midway to the Hawaiian islands to detect American ship movements, but owing to the advance intelligence the carriers have already moved past this point, ready to launch.

In the northern Pacific, aerial groups from Japanese carriers *Ryujo* and *Junyo* bomb Dutch Harbor in the Aleutian Islands. Knowing this attack to be a diversion for the main Midway operation, the US Navy sends a force of five cruisers and four destroyers, but retains the majority of its strength in the central Pacific.

2

3

4

5

04.30: Chuichi Nagumo – in tactical command of the force at sea as he had been at Pearl Harbor – launches the first planned attack on Midway. A group of 36 dive bombers, 36 torpedo bombers and 36 fighters aims to neutralise land-based defences on the island, as well as prevent US aircraft from using the airstrips during the planned invasion.

04.32: Japanese search aircraft take to the skies, but the Navy's reconnaissance missions are poorly planned and under-equipped with only eight aircraft operating over huge radius.

05.34: Eleven PBYs from Midway report seeing two Japanese carriers, and also spot the incoming air strike.

06.20: Nagumo's aerial group bombs the US base at Midway causing extensive damage, but crucially does not manage to halt operations at the facility. American bombers are still able to use the airfield, and anti-aircraft guns are unaffected. Japanese pilots report to Nagumo on their return that a second strike is needed if the invasion is to occur on June 7 as planned.

07.00: The first aircraft begin taking off from the US aircraft carriers, but a lack of experience in launching such vast operations means the groups are far slower at getting into the air than the Japanese. Throughout the next hour, 67 dive bombers, 29 torpedo bombers and 20 fighters head for the reported positions of Yamamoto's fleet.

07.10: US aircraft from Midway Island begin attack runs on the Japanese fleet, but are repelled by enemy fighters scoring no significant hits.

07.15: Following Japanese carrier tactical protocol of the time, Nagumo has kept half of his aircraft back in case any American ships are discovered. With land-based attacks from Midway coming in waves, and on the recommendation of his pilots about a second strike, Nagumo orders that his reserve aircraft be re-armed with payloads intended for ground strikes.

07.40: Frenetic work continues aboard the carriers to change the weaponry as a delayed scout plane returns with a sighting of an American naval force to the east. The American ambush has worked and Nagumo is surprised by the presence of so many Pacific Fleet vessels which he had believed to still be stationed in the South Pacific. He has to reverse his snap decision, and orders another scouting effort to determine the exact composition of the US group. It takes between 20 and 40 minutes for word to come through that a carrier is present; the delay and subsequent indecision having created havoc on board the four Japanese carriers.

<u>**6**</u>

1. Japanese bombardment of Midway caused significant damage to buildings on the island. ✪
2. Buildings at Dutch Harbor, Aleutian Islands, in flames after a Japanese air offensive. ✪
3. An explosion rocks Dutch Harbor. ✪
4. At Sand Island in the Midway Atoll an oil tank burns as the result of Japanese air attack. ✪
5. A seaplane hangar at Midway's US base burns after being struck during the morning raids. ✪
6. The US Navy had worked out that the Japanese invasion of the Aleutian Islands was intended as a diversion, and so was only able to commit a notional force to its defence. Members of that force are pictured as they lie in wait for Japanese aircraft to appear. ✪

The Battle of Midway
America devastates the Japanese fleet

As chaos reigns on Nagumo's ships and in the air above, American aircraft from carriers *Hornet, Enterprise* and *Yorktown* begin to arrive. The US approach is certainly not tactically perfect, with staggered launches meaning the various attack groups arrive at different times. The first attackers also struggle to locate their targets, some having initially followed an incorrect bearing, and because the aircraft had taken so long to launch some run low on fuel and have to turn back.

This is indeed the case for the Wildcat fighter escorts of a squadron from *Hornet* that reaches its intended destination at 9.20am without cover. The bombers commence attack runs at 9.40am, but all 15 TBD Devastators are shot down without even getting close to the Japanese carriers. Of the group's 30 crewmembers, only ensign George H Gay Jr survives. Ten Devastators from *Enterprise* and a further 12 from *Yorktown* are also destroyed. This will be the last time the vulnerable Devastator is used in combat – the terrible performance of their Mark 13 torpedoes also being a significant factor.

Despite the initial sorties' apparent lack of success, the four Japanese carriers have taken evasive action and are now scattered. It is the same story for Japan's aerial groups – a lack of communication and planning leaves the defensive fighters out of position and short on fuel and ammunition. A brief period of quiet in the skies allows crews on board *Akagi, Kaga, Soryu* and *Hiryu* to attempt some form of organisation, but the rush to refuel and arm aircraft has left oil tanks, hoses, torpedoes and other weapons exposed on deck – along with the men undertaking the work.

By 10am a *Yorktown* squadron is approaching from the south-east, and by chance so are three further groups – two from *Enterprise* and one more of *Yorktown* – from the south-west and north-east. *Enterprise's* two aerial forces are running low on fuel but by good fortune spot the trail of the destroyer *Arashi* heading back towards the Japanese carriers and the squadron's commander Clarence Wade McClusky Jr decides to pursue. Some aircraft run out of fuel and are lost, but McClusky's aggressiveness means that all four squadrons are in a position to launch a surprise attack together.

At 10.22am the two *Enterprise*-based forces separate with the aim of attacking both *Akagi* and *Kaga*, but a miscommunication means both dive at the

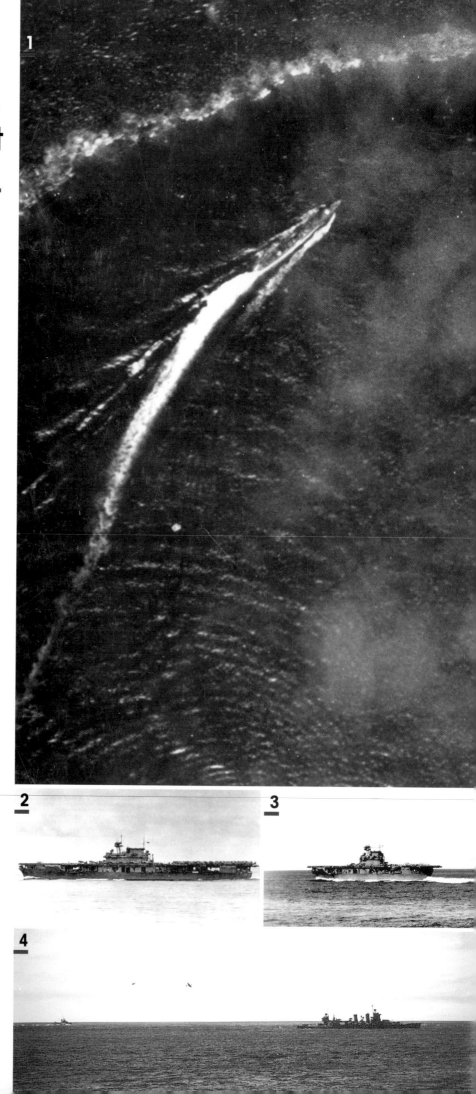

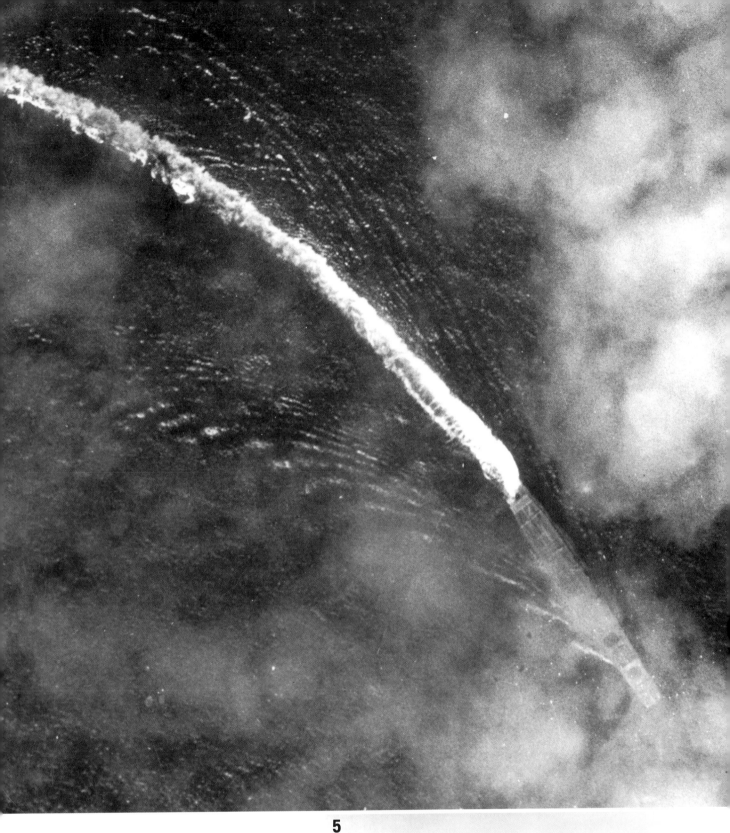

5

1. Japan's flag carrier *Akagi* manoeuvres below thin cloud while under attack from US Army Air Forces B-17 bombers early on June 4. The USAAF would later take credit for America's victory at Midway, but these raids were largely ineffectual – it was the later carrier strikes that made the difference. ✪
2. USS *Yorktown* under way early on June 4. ✪
3. A fast-moving USS *Enterprise* is seen from USS *Pensacola*. SBD aircraft below the carrier deck are being prepared for re-spotting the flight deck; the squadrons already in flight are the ones that will fatally damage *Akagi* and *Kaga*. ✪
4. Cruiser USS *Astoria* stops to pick up a downed SBD crew which is about to ditch into the ocean. Many aircraft from America's deadly first attack stretched their fuel range to the absolute maximum, and several still didn't have enough to make it back to their home carriers. ✪
5. A US Navy Douglas Dauntless scout bomber returns to *Yorktown* after its role in the attack on Japanese carrier *Kaga*. ✪

latter. Under a terrific onslaught from the feared Dauntless dive bomber, *Kaga* is the victim of at least four direct hits which inflict heavy damage and ignite several fires.

Realising that both squadrons were descending on the same target, Lieutenant Commander Richard Halsey Best and his two wingmen had managed to pull out of the run and direct their focus to *Akagi*. A matter of minutes after *Kaga's* been mauled, Best hits the Japanese flagship and although she only suffers one bomb strike it proves to be a fatal blow as it lands and explodes among the armed and fuelled aircraft at the upper hangar deck.

Next it's the turn of *Yorktown's* group, which swarms all over *Soryu*. She is hit with at least three bombs, and other aircraft that have mistakenly jettisoned their payloads en route strafe the deck. Fuel on board quickly ignites, while piles of bombs and other ammunition detonate to make the situation even more threatening. *Hiryu* is also targeted at this time, but the final squadron from *Yorktown* is unable to land a blow.

Within just six minutes, *Soryu* and *Kaga* are burning from stern to stern and fires are raging throughout both ships at an incredible speed. *Akagi*, having suffered just one bomb hit, takes longer to succumb but fires on the vessel prove just as damaging and are impossible extinguish. It takes the remainder of the day and into the next morning, but eventually all three carriers are consumed by the fires and crews are forced to abandon them before they are scuttled. In one fell swoop, *Akagi*, *Soryu* and *Kaga* have been lost to the Japanese fleet.

1. Like *Akagi*, *Soryu* came under attack from B-17 bombers early in the day, before the Dauntless dive bombers were unleashed. She's pictured circling as an evasive move – the circular wake about 1160m in diameter. ✪
2. Wildcat fighters and Dauntless dive bombers prepare to launch from the flight deck of USS *Hornet*. ✪
3. Launching from USS *Yorktown*, a Wildcat fighter takes off for a defensive combat air patrol. ✪
4. An SBD returns to *Hornet* from an attack run during the ongoing battle. ✪
5. A view from cruiser USS *Penscola*, one of the many Pacific Fleet ships supporting America's Midway operation. ✪
6. Japanese carrier *Kaga* steams ahead of *Zuikaku* as the two prepare for the previous year's attack on Pearl Harbor. The destruction of *Kaga* at Midway, along with four of the other six ships which launched aircraft against Hawaii on December 7, is a stunning and poignant victory for the US Navy. ✪
7. Two SBD-3s stalk already burning Japanese ships below. ✪

The Battle of Midway
The death of USS *Yorktown*
BEGINNING AT 11:00, JUNE 4 |

Having managed to survive America's
swift and brutal strike, *Hiryu* is ordered to
launch an immediate counterattack and its
planes set off in pursuit of the withdrawing
US squadrons. Its first wave consists of 18
dive bombers and six fighters and, acting
on little more than a thirst for revenge, they
strike the first carrier they find – *Yorktown*.
At 12.05pm a hole is blown in her deck,
her boilers halted and an anti-aircraft gun
destroyed by three successful bomb hits.
The damage is such that Fletcher is forced
to transfer his command staff onto the
heavy cruiser *Astoria*.

1. The damage from Japanese aerial raids
   shows aboard USS *Yorktown*.✪

1

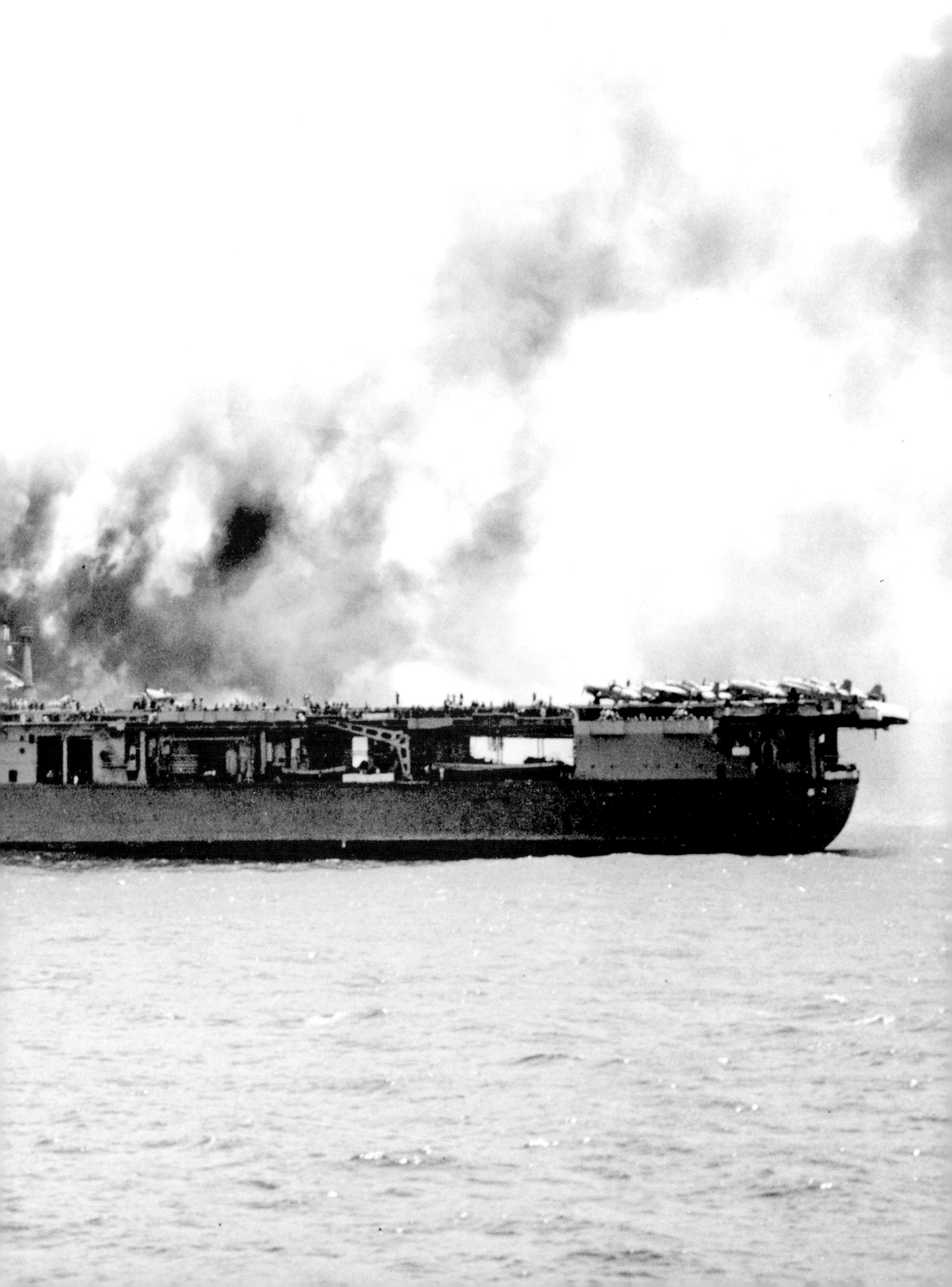

Repair teams work feverishly and somehow manage to patch up *Yorktown* – already less than 100% fit after the Battle of the Coral Sea – within an hour. She is recovered to such a degree that she is able to continue air operations and welcomes back returning crews from the day's action before preparing them to relaunch and seek out Japan's one remaining carrier in operation at Midway.

By 4pm a fully manoeuvring *Yorktown* is under way at 20 knots, and has sent fighters to intercept a group of incoming enemy planes that have been detected on radar. The attack is courtesy of *Hiryu's* second wave and consists of 10 B5N torpedo bombers and six escorting fighters, but while *Yorktown's* Wildcats are able shoot down three Kates the others push past into a heavy barrage of anti-aircraft fire. *Yorktown* has to move radically to avoid at least two torpedo hits, but a further two strike her within minutes of each other. The carrier loses power and goes dead in the water as she lists to port.

The crew manages to extinguish all boiler fires, but without power there is no way to correct the list and all on board are advised to make preparations for evacuation. At an angle of 26° the ship's commander and engineering officer agree that capsize is imminent and order that the ship be abandoned. Making a final tour, the pair ensure that no crew remain on board and are the last to leave just as water begins to lap on to the port side of the hangar deck.

To everyone's surprise, *Yorktown* remains afloat throughout the night after the battle and so plans are drawn up to begin a salvage operation. On the morning of June 6, a group of five destroyers form a screen around the stricken vessel to protect against Japanese submarines, and a salvage party board the carrier to begin repairs and rescue. The salvage progresses well in the afternoon; with topside weight reduced the list decreased by two degrees.

Unknown to the six destroyers and *Yorktown*, a Japanese submarine sneaks close enough to engage and fires two torpedoes – one hits USS *Hammann* and she goes down rapidly – while two strike *Yorktown*. About a minute after *Hammann* sinks an underwater explosion kills many of the crew from her and *Yorktown* who have been thrown into the water, and causes further damage to the already stricken carrier. The remaining destroyers launch a frantic search for the submarine but the Japanese vessel disappears, so attention is focused on rescuing survivors and further attempts to salvage *Yorktown*.

Remarkably, *Yorktown* remains afloat still as the sun rises on the morning of June 7, but observers note that her list has increased rapidly.

At 7.01pm the beleaguered old warrior finally relents, turns over onto her port side, rolls upside-down and sinks into the 5500m of ocean below.

1. USS *Yorktown's* crew abandon ship. Destroyer USS *Balch* is standing by to pick up those in the water, as inflatable life rafts are deployed off the carrier's stern. ✪
2. A Japanese torpedo aircraft (top right) from carrier *Hiryu* closes on *Yorktown*. ✪
3. Gunners on *Yorktown* prepare for further Japanese raids as smoke pours from the ship behind them. ✪
4. Crew aboard the damaged Yorktown attempt to put out fires. ✪
5. Smoke billows from *Yorktown* after Japanese bomb strikes. ✪
6. Having already abandoned ship, survivors from *Yorktown* are picked up by USS *Hammann* and other escort ships. The carrier is now listing more than 20°. ✪

1. Firefighters in USS *Yorktown's* hangar attempt to tackle intense blazes. ✿
2. Admiral Frank Fletcher prepares to board USS *Astoria* having been forced to vacate his damaged flagship. ✿
3. *Yorktown* sailors prepare to abandon the rapidly listing ship. ✿
4. *Yorktown* survivors check in aboard rescue vessel USS *Fulton*. ✿
5. After a sustained attack, *Yorktown* is left dead in the water. ✿
6. Heavy cruiser USS *Portland*, right, transfers *Yorktown* survivors to the submarine tender *Fulton* on June 7. ✿
7. Despite remaining afloat against all odds, and as salvage looked a more and more likely proposition, *Yorktown* finally goes down having been torpedoed by a Japanese submarine. ✿
8. The destroyer USS *Benham* with 720 survivors from *Yorktown* on board. ✿
9. A photographer manages to catch the moment just before *Hammann* goes under following a Japanese submarine torpedo strike while she assisted with the attempted salvage of *Yorktown*. ✿

The Battle of Midway
Cementing a US victory
BEGINNING AT 13:30 |

Early in the afternoon, a *Yorktown* scout spots Japan's one remaining carrier operating at Midway and so *Enterprise* sends a final force of 24 dive bombers – some from the damaged *Yorktown* – in a bid to finish the job. *Hiryu* only has four airworthy dive bombers and five torpedo planes remaining and is vulnerable, yet Yamamoto orders Nagumo to launch a third strike to find and destroy the American carriers – Japan's premier admiral intent on winning a decisive battle.

Nagumo has already ordered his fleet to retreat westwards, but at 4.45pm the American dive bombers spot the mighty Japanese vessel and close in. Just after 5pm, even though she's defended by a group of at least 10 Zero fighters, the *Enterprise* and *Yorktown* aircraft hit *Hiryu* with four 1000lb bombs and the huge blasts create fires across the deck.

While *Hiryu's* power is not affected, the crew is unable to control the fires on board. Eventually her engines give out, then just before midnight a huge explosion rocks the ship and causes additional damage. The order to abandon ship is given at 3.15am and survivors are evacuated by two Japanese destroyers. One of those destroyers, *Makigumo*, is tasked with scuttling *Hiryu*; flag officer Vice Admiral Tamon Yamaguchi and her captain Tomeo Kaku choose to go down with their ship.

The torpedo strike intended to sink *Hiryu*, however, is unsuccessful and at 7am an aircraft from light carrier *Hosho* discovers her still afloat and not in any visible danger of sinking. Crewmen are still visible aboard the deck and rush to launch boats – 39 managing to do so before *Hiryu* does eventually succumb at 9.12am. The bodies of 389 crew go down with her.

Action continues for several days, but the sinking of *Hiryu* represents the last of the major engagements, and Japan is left counting the cost of losing four carriers from its powerful and previously all-conquering Combined Fleet.

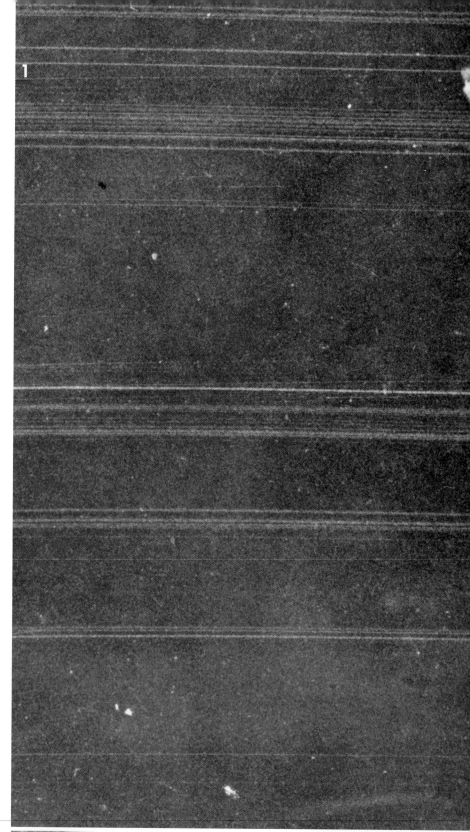

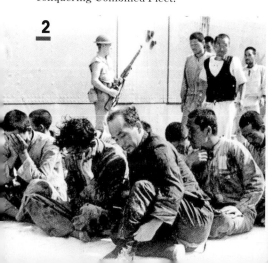

4

1. *Hiryu* was subjected to bombing by B-17 aircraft early in the day, but clearly the payloads have landed to her right. ✪

2. Japanese prisoners of war under guard on Midway after they were rescued from an open lifeboat by destroyer USS *Ballard*. This group were among 35 survivors from *Hiryu* picked up by *Ballard* on June 14. ✪

3. Another shot of *Hiryu* burning on the morning of June 5, prior to her sinking. ✪

4. *Hiryu*, as pictured by a Yokosuka B4Y aircraft of carrier *Hosho* shortly after sunrise on June 5. Japanese destroyers had attempted to scuttle the ship with torpedoes the night before, but she refused to sink – eventually going under a few hours after this photograph was taken. ✪

JUNE 4 |

As night falls, both sides consider making further efforts to inflict damage. Initially Yamamoto decides to continue with the invasion effort but fails to make contact with any American forces. The US carriers and their escorts have been withdrawn west as US Navy leaders know Japan holds the advantage if a night-time battle ensues.

JUNE 5 |

At sea Nagumo is forced to begin the clean-up operation, and has to scuttle Japan's premier carrier *Akagi*. In the early hours of the morning Yamamoto orders the proposed night assault on Midway to be cancelled, and then at 2.25am calls a halt to Operation MI entirely. US aircraft and submarines chase remaining Japanese ships in the area, and the panic causes a collision between heavy cruisers *Mogami* and *Mikuma*. At 10.24pm, a Japanese submarine surfaces just off the coast of Midway and fires its guns without inflicting any damage.

JUNE 6 |

Attack aircraft from *Enterprise* and *Hornet* locate a group of Japanese vessels and damage the destroyers *Arashio* and *Asashi* as well as *Mogami*. Fatal blows are also struck against *Mikuma*, and 650 perish on board when she sinks later in the day. The American fleet withdraws to the east to refuel, effectively bringing the battle to a close.

JUNE 7 |

Saratoga has now arrived and transfers aircraft to *Enterprise* and *Hornet* so they can continue operations and sail north in defence of the Aleutian Islands. However, after bombing campaigns in the previous days Japanese troops occupy Kiska.

JUNE 8 |

Two battleships, one escort carrier and two heavy cruisers depart Japan's retreating Midway force to support the Aleutian campaign.

JUNE 9 |

Fletcher is now commanding the fleet from the *Saratoga*, and continues to launch sorties to ensure the Japanese group is no longer advancing on Midway Island.

JUNE 10 |

American air patrols discover that Japanese troops have successfully invaded Kiska and Attu in the Aleutians. Meanwhile, as news of the Midway engagement begins to spread, the Japanese information bureau announces that only one of its carriers was lost in the battle while two US vessels were sunk. Back in the Pacific, Fletcher determines that the threat of invasion no longer remains and pulls back his carriers. The fleet will shortly return to Pearl Harbor.

1. The sole surviving TBF-1 Avenger of *Hornet* torpedo squadron is pictured on Midway in late June. ✪
2. Aircraft carrier USS *Saratoga* arrives at Pearl Harbor on June 6, ready to steam towards Midway and support the still ongoing naval engagement. ✪
3. Troops of the Japanese Special Naval Landing Force raise the country's naval ensign on Kiska Island in the Aleutians. ✪
4. Injured, exhausted – or possibly both – a US Navy PBY-5 Catalina crewmember is taken out of his aircraft on a stretcher on Midway after the battle. ✪
5. A close-up shot of Japanese destroyer *Mogami* shows the damage inflicted by US aerial attack groups. ✪
6. Ensign George Gay, part of the only surviving Avenger's crew, was also the only man of the group to make it back to *Hornet*. He's pictured shortly after the battle, reading about his country's emphatic victory. ✪

As the action at Midway subsided, the US fleet emphasised its crushing victory by chasing down Yamamoto's retreating ships and inflicting further losses on the already battered force. One such example was the cruiser *Mikuma*, pictured burning shortly before she sank on June 6. Japan had gambled at Pearl Harbor and won, but Midway proved to be a risk too far and its forces were comprehensively defeated. They returned to its territories and home islands, attempting to evade further American attacks and assess substantial losses. ✪

CHAPTER 11

THE PACIFIC WAR AFTER MIDWAY

As the two forces retired to friendlier waters after the Battle of Midway, the scale of America's victory over Japan quickly began to emerge. There was little doubt about it, the Pacific War had dramatically shifted course...

Japan was left reeling in the days and weeks after Midway; not even in his worst nightmares had Yamamoto envisioned such a comprehensive and decisive defeat. The body count totalled a staggering 3058 – more than had been killed at Pearl Harbor.

The heaviest losses occured on the four fleet carriers – *Akagi*, 267; *Kaga,* 811; *Hiryu*, 392; *Soryu*, 711. The total of US dead, from the sinking of USS *Yorktown* and USS *Hammann*, came to 307.

In the cold hard reality of warfare, America's casualties were replaceable but Japan's 2181 dead carrier crewmen had been experienced, well-trained and battle-hardened. In fact, the Japanese deaths at Midway included 40% of the fleet's trained

aircraft mechanics and technicians, plus flight-deck crew and armourers, and the loss of these men's combined operational knowledge would be among the most damaging blows inflicted on the Japanese throughout the entire Pacific War.

On June 15, Admiral Nagumo submitted his battle report to the high command – the closely guarded document accessible only to the upper echelons of the Japanese system – and in it he stated that "the enemy is not aware of our plans." Even after such a crushing and unexpected defeat, he did not realise that his operation had unravelled thanks to the efforts of American code breakers at Station HYPO, and it was an ignorance that would continue to haunt the Japanese war effort in the years to come.

Japanese news of the day reported that its forces had won a great victory at Midway, and only Emperor Hirohito and the Japanese Navy high command were privy to the accurate and far more sobering details. Even the Imperial Army continued under the assumption, for a period at least, that the Combined Fleet was fully operational.

As the wounded were returned to the home islands they were transferred to Navy hospitals and classified as 'secret' patients – quarantined from fellow troops and even their own families in case they revealed the true nature of the events that had occurred in the central Pacific.

Japan quickly pushed new pilots through a condensed training programme in order to more quickly replenish the number of

Allied forces prepare to embark the beaches of Guadalcanal. ✪

Japanese Navy Type 1 land attack planes, later code named 'Betty' by the Allies, fly low through anti-aircraft fire during a torpedo attack on Allied ships off the coast of Guadalcanal. ✪

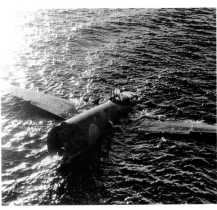

The largely intact wreckage of a Betty bomber which crashed during Japan's attack on the Allied invasion force. ✪

available airmen, but this inevitably led to a decline in the quality of naval aviators coming through the ranks. The weary survivors were given no time to rest or recover, and were forced to accept an increased share of the operational workload due to the shortages.

Given this situation it seemed that Japan's only option would be to immediately go on the defensive. But rather than take time to reflect on defeat and mount a measured response, its forces continued to be deployed on risky – even foolhardy – missions in the now key territories of New Guinea and the Solomon Islands off Australia's northern coast. Tactically, Midway had been an anomaly – a desperate effort by Yamamoto to achieve his

much-vaunted final battle scenario. The much more consistent focus of Japanese operations was defeating the US by isolating Australia, and all efforts were refocused on achieving this aim.

From region to region, island to island, Japan had appeared unstoppable before the battles at Coral Sea and Midway but now, without adequate air cover, crucial weaknesses came to the fore and a revitalised Allied force was ready and waiting to capitalise on them.

In August, just two months on from its stunning victory at Midway, the US committed a sizeable group of US troops to the first Allied offensive of the Pacific War against the Empire of Japan. The chosen target was Guadalcanal.

While several more concurrent operations would launch on the island of New Guinea, in the Solomons and on other outlying territories in the region, the action on Guadalcanal came to symbolise this particular period of the Pacific Theatre. It was a time during which the opposing sides were perhaps at their most well-matched. If anything, Japan still held the advantage in terms of strength and numbers.

America, however, had the all-important momentum, and was able to outmanoeuvre the increasingly ragged Japanese military branches to neutralise any threat that remained of a potential isolation or invasion of Australia.

Once that was achieved, attention turned to the Japanese home islands.

A Japanese aircraft burns on the water after being shot down attempting to attack US transport vessels between Guadalcanal and Tulagi. ✪

Scores of dead Japanese soldiers lie on the sand at the mouth of Alligator Creek, Guadalcanal, on August 21. ✪

The Guadalcanal campaign

Guadalcanal, a damp and mosquito-ridden jungle, had been largely ignored by the Japanese before construction of its airfield began. The Americans had not been interested either, but when intelligence efforts revealed that the Imperial Navy was developing a facility there the 2000 square mile island mass became one of the Pacific War's most hotly contested areas.

On August 7 the US First Marine Division mounted a successful, albeit amateurish, amphibious landing with the intention of assuming control of the air base being built by the Japanese. It was one of America's first ever assaults of this kind and the landers arrived without knowledge of the terrain, the tide or the weather – all of which were relatively unfavourable to them. Nevertheless, by 9.10am two battalions totalling 11,000 troops established advantageous positions on the coastline and overwhelmed the outnumbered Japanese defenders to occupy the base. Later that month, the airstrip was named Henderson Field in honour of Marine Major Lofton Henderson who was the first marine aviator killed during the Battle of Midway.

Unlike the previously clear-cut engagements such as those in the Coral Sea and at Midway, this initial incursion proved to be just a prelude for a months-long military operation during which there would be several skirmishes as Japan looked to retake the air strip and surrounding buildings. It was a hellish time for both sides; with little infrastructure in place, dysentery spread quickly and the respective threats from the sea forces of both Japan and America meant both were unable to

LEFT: The terrain and conditions encountered by the Marines were far from familiar. And with patrols such as this one, it's easy to see how tropical diseases spread among the forces. ✪

A wounded US Marine is evacuated during fighting at Guadalcanal's Koli Point in November 1942. ✪

A US Marine Corps amphibian tractor moves up the beach on Guadalcanal during American landings on the island in early August. ✪

The wreckage of an SBD scout bomber, still burning after it was destroyed by a Japanese air attack on Henderson Field. ✪

Weary US Marines rest in a field during Guadalcanal operations. ✪

ship supplies to their troops which resulted in rationing.

During the course of the elongated campaign there were three major land battles, seven large naval battles and constant aerial bombardments, but none resulted in a major victory or defeat and none were able to break America's hold on Henderson Field.

Japan's Army and Navy had committed significant resource and manpower to recapturing the Guadalcanal base, but the cost of its continued failure was beginning to mount and early in the month a group of 7000 infantrymen was dispatched for one final push. In anticipation of their landing, several Japanese warships were instructed to launch a sustained assault on Henderson from the sea to destroy Allied aircraft that might pose a threat to the convoy. American intelligence was once again able to intercede, however, and the Allies gathered a naval force to counter the planned attack on its airfield and set about preventing Japanese troops from ever reaching Guadalcanal.

Aircraft carrier USS *Wasp* burning and listing after she was torpedoed by a Japanese submarine during operations in support of American forces on Guadalcanal. The danger posed by such missions meant US Navy support for the island was difficult and led to a shortage of equipment and rations. ✪

A 75mm pack howitzer and its US Marine crew are pictured deep in the Guadalcanal jungle in September or October 1942. ✪

Both sides lost several warships in the resulting hostilities, but the end result was America turning back Japan's coastline bombardment group and the sinking of the majority of its transport convoys. Before the end of the year the Japanese high command had approved the evacuation of its remaining Guadalcanal personnel in order to create a new defensive line in the Solomon Islands and shift its depleted resources to the ongoing campaign to retain control of New Guinea.

In practical terms, America's ability to remain steadfast resulted in Guadalcanal becoming a major supporting base for further Allied offensives up through the Solomon Islands and towards New Guinea.

Japan pulled back, vital equipment and experienced fighters that it could ill afford to lose having been bled away. Estimates put the number of Japanese group troops killed at Guadalcanal at 25,000 – as many as three-quarters succumbing to non-combat causes of death such as starvation or tropical disease.

As Japan finally reverted to defending its Pacific perimeter rather than attempting to further extend its influence, it no longer had the necessary resources to undertake what was still a monumental task.

"Get Yamamoto"

The Japanese tactic of continued aggressive action after the defeat at Midway was driven largely by Yamamoto's determination not to be pushed back into a defensive stance. It was he who proposed – even demanded – a continuation of his aggressive policies and advocated the speeding up of construction at Guadalcanal airfield before it was swiftly ripped from Japanese control.

Even after the further setback, Yamamoto was convinced – as he had been at Midway – that he could draw the American carrier fleet out in defence of Henderson Field, and this was a driving force behind the multiple attempts by the Japanese Navy and Army to retake the strategic location. The US, however, would not be tempted. The Pacific Fleet carrier group had only steamed into action in the Coral Sea and Midway because the US Navy knew it held the advantage having learned of Japanese intentions beforehand through intelligence gathering.

Otherwise, there was simply no way Nimitz would leave his premier vessels prone to Japanese counteroffensives – particularly when considering that his mightiest battleships were still undergoing salvage at Pearl Harbor and on the American west coast. Instead the bulk of American forces remained safely behind a strong defensive line, enabling them to launch a string of smaller attacks against Japanese positions on Guadalcanal and other nearby areas. The sum total of these engagements would prove just as damaging to Japan as the explosive naval action of the summer months.

By February 1943, any Japanese hopes of recapturing Guadalcanal had been completely extinguished, and the once revered Yamamoto finally lost the confidence of the Naval General Staff. He could not convince them that Japan should remain on the front foot – it simply no longer possessed that capability after the defeat of its carrier group and losses incurred attempting to win back Henderson – and he was left with no other option but to comply with the traditional defensive doctrine. Now unable to exert any great influence, Yamamoto departed for a morale-boosting tour of the South Pacific territories where he hoped to cajole his country's troops into redoubling their efforts to try and fend off the reinvigorated Americans. It would be the admiral's last move.

American code-breakers – Station HYPO officers among them – managed to intercept and decrypt orders alerting various Japanese units with details of the tour. They discovered that Yamamoto would be flying from Rabaul to Balalae Airfeld, on a small island near Bougainville in the Solomon Islands, on April 18.

The information made its way through the chain of command, eventually reaching President Roosevelt; the commander-in-chief giving the order to American Navy Secretary Frank Knox: "Get Yamamoto."

A US Navy SBD-3 flies over carrier USS Enterprise off Guadalcanal in December 1942. By this time, America had established firm control of the region, although it's likely that the aircraft is on anti-submarine patrol. ✪

The crashed remains of Yamamoto's G4M transport in the jungle of Bougainville, discovered the day after it was shot down. ✪

Yamamoto's ashes return to Japan having been transported aboard the battleship *Musashi*. ✪

The de facto assassination of an individual political or armed services figurehead by another country was unprecedented in the modern world, but Roosevelt knew how important Yamamoto was in Japan and what his death would represent to its naval forces. After the destruction of carriers that launched against Pearl Harbor on December 7, it also offered the tantalising prospect of enacting final revenge for the Hawaiian raid.

The mission would be known as Operation Vengeance and, as it made its way back down the rungs of US naval authority, Nimitz gave the final go-ahead for a squadron of Lockheed P-38 Lightning aircraft to intercept Yamamoto's touring party. Discovering the target as anticipated, the 16 Lightnings engaged the six Zero

fighter escorts and the two Mitsubishi G4M bombers – being used as transports – in the skies over Bougainville at just after 9.30am. The first G4M hit was the one carrying Japan's famous admiral and after being struck by gunfire smoke poured from its left-side engine before it crashed into the dense jungle below.

Search planes made desperate attempts to find survivors, and it would take a land-based rescue group until the following day to locate the wreckage where they discovered Yamamoto's body. He was still upright in his seat under a tree, his hand grasping the hilt of his katana, but two .50 calibre bullets had hit him – one in the back of his left shoulder and the other entering through his left lower jaw before exiting above his right eye.

When Japan released the details of incident on May 21, though not the detail of Yamamoto's fatal injuries, the news created shock and sadness across the country while simultaneously providing a major injection of morale for both Americans at home and those fighting overseas.

In the US, to cover up the fact that the Allies were intercepted and understanding Japanese code, American news agencies were given the same cover story that had been relayed to the fighter squadron that had undertaken the mission: civilian coastwatchers in the Solomons had observed Yamamoto boarding a bomber and relayed the information to American naval forces in the immediate area. Japan believed that the discovery had been nothing more than a stroke of bad luck.

Midway's wider impact

The Guadalcanal campaign showed that the US had grasped what naval doctrine describes as the "operational initiative", and after Midway it was Japan reacting to American offensives rather than the other way around.

And this wasn't just true of the Pacific Theatre, with the US defeat of the Combined Fleet giving a welcome boost to the Allies' worldwide approach.

At the start of May 1942, the outlook for the Allied forces had been bleak. Germany's army was dominant in Europe, a German-Italian force was closing on the Suez Canal and the Japanese had ravaged the Pacific Fleet before driving the British out of the Indian Ocean and some of its Asian colonies.

Japan was even threatening to link up with the Germans in the Middle East – and had the Axis powers had been able to reach each other's imperial boundaries it would have spelled disaster for the vital British and American supply line through Iran.

The Russians were beleaguered as they struggled to prevent the Germans from seizing Moscow, there was every possibility that the battered Chinese forces would look to negotiate a cease-fire with Japan if they were cut off from American aid and Britain faced a revolt in India that might end its jurisdiction there, leaving easy pickings for Japan, Germany or both.

It was a dire situation, to say the least, and the Allied countries desperately needed something to limit the sheer number of fronts on which they were fighting – Midway turned out to be that something. Such was the setback that Japan had suffered, it had to concentrate its efforts on Guadalcanal and the wider Solomon Islands and New Guinea. There was no longer a sustained threat in Asia, particularly to India where Japan never realistically possessed the strength to reignite its campaign in Burma.

As Roosevelt and British Prime Minister Winston Churchill came together for the Casablanca Conference in January 1943 they were, for the first time, able to commit to coordinating global Allied offensives rather than just having to fire-fight potential or actual invasions and occupations. The major outcome of the meeting was the decision to hold firm in the Pacific while concentrating Allied strength on efforts against Germany; this would subsequently draw the Nazis away from the eastern front, easing pressure on the Soviet Union and allowing room for its forces to regroup and counterattack.

An invasion of Sicily and the Italian mainland was designed to knock Italy out of the war, and while this was being achieved forces would be bolstered in England for an eventual attempt to establish a foothold in

President Roosevelt and Prime Minister Churchill are flanked by their advisors at the 1943 Casablanca Conference. ✪

northern France. As the Allies' power increased and America's industrial might began to tell, there would also be an effort to entirely eject Japan from New Guinea.

On the final day of the conference Roosevelt announced that he and Churchill would pursue a policy of unconditional surrender as the only way to ensure a postwar peace. He stressed that this would not mean the annihilation of Axis populations, but rather "the destruction of the philosophies in those countries which are based on conquest and the subjugation of other people".

CHAPTER 12

A SYMBOLIC BATTLE IN THE SKIES

Several aircraft types made their mark in the Pacific War, but there were three that came to perfectly encapsulate the Theatre: Japan's Mitsubishi Zero fighter, and America's Grumman Wildcat fighter and Douglas Dauntless dive bomber. It's not that this trio were the most successful (although in some aspects they were) and it's not because they were the most produced (although in some instances that was the case). Rather, the story of each was eerily symbolic of the actions and fortunes of the country it represented...

The fearsome yet flawed Zero

For the first six months of the war, the Mitsubishi A6M fighter was simply untouchable. While America had taken numerous steps to avoid confrontation in the Pacific, Japan had been actively preparing for military operations outside of its borders and so had been developing the equipment necessary for success. The Zero fighter was one such piece of equipment.

Other manufacturers had said it couldn't be done, but Mitsubishi managed to produce one of the most agile aircraft of its kind. Quick and nimble, the Zero was able to outperform almost anything it encountered – if it couldn't outrun them then it could outmanoeuvre them with a turning circle that defied the accepted notions of what was possible in aircraft design of the time. Despite the dominance it demonstrated in the late 1930s, and the fact that it had clearly been produced for a purpose, America and other western powers offered little in the way of a reaction. When Japanese forces, the Zero included, devastated the US Pacific Fleet at Pearl Harbor the rest of the world was left playing

A6M2 and A6M3 Zeros from *Zuikaku* prepare for a mission at Rabaul. ✪

A Model 22 Zero in flight over the Solomon Islands in 1943. ✪

catch-up. For all of its early success, however, the Zero had inherent weaknesses that would eventually bring about its downfall. Striving for quick gains rather than giving full consideration to all aspects of aerial warfare, designers had stripped all excess weight from the fighter to enhance its flying capabilities. Among the weighty items it lacked were vital armour and self-sealing fuel tanks.

As America made tactical and operational gains against Japan in 1942, an intact A6M was captured during the Aleutian campaign and was carefully studied to see what made it tick. It soon became clear that the brilliant and feared Zero was actually highly vulnerable.

Just as the Allied code breaking had given America the advantage at sea, this crucial analysis gave US pilots the edge in the air. Rather than engaging in the lost cause of an aerial dogfight, their bulkier and more powerful aircraft could get above the Zero and descend with a short and accurate burst of fire. This was often enough to cause fatal damage given the lack of protection.

The Zero represented the Japanese qualities of ingenuity, craftsmanship and determination, and for a short time there was not an aircraft in the world that could even hope to rival it. But once its key weakness was discovered and its enemies learned how to fight it effectively, its domination came to an end.

The resilient and efficient Dauntless

An SBD-5 Dauntless, bomb clearly visible, in flight over Wake Island in October 1943. ✪

Douglas's SBD dive bomber began the Pacific War having been declared obsolete, yet ended the conflict with the more enemy ships sunk to its name than all other US Navy aircraft combined and more than any other single aircraft in the Pacific Theatre. While Japan had found success from acts of brilliance – the development of the Zero or the audacious raid in Hawaii, for example – it soon became clear that America's progress would rely on its sheer efficiency.

The Dauntless was the epitome of this approach. It had no frills, no extraordinary capabilities; it simply excelled at what it was designed for, and that was dive-bombing. Starting at an altitude of 2000-3000ft the pilot would cut the throttle, gently fall into a 70-degree descent, extend the air brakes and at around 800ft release the payload.

Once the ordnance was clear, it was time to pull the nose up, retract the brakes, hit the throttle and climb quickly away from the target below. The Dauntless suffered from a weak underbelly, but was capable of flying at tree-top level; or if it was engaged at altitude it could out-dive most potential attackers. Everything about it was produced with machine-like precision.

Its capabilities came to the fore at Coral Sea and Midway where the Dauntless was at its most devastating. For all Japan's technical advances and intricate military tactics, its Combined Fleet simply had no answer to the rain of fire unleashed from the relentless dive bomber squadrons.

Dauntless domination continued in the months and years after as the type wreaked havoc on any concentration of Japanese

The plucky and reliable Wildcat

The Grumman F4F was not an aircraft necessarily ready or equipped for every eventuality. It was capable, it filled a need and most importantly it was ready when hostilities ensued, but on first inspection it appeared to have little chance of standing up to the Zero.

Wildcats were first used in anger in the attempted defence of Wake Island, and they showed signs of the resilience that would be displayed for the rest of the conflict by managing to delay Japan's inevitable conquest of the territory by contributing to the sinking of two enemy destroyers – *Kisaragi* and *Hayate*.

Despite its early show of strength however, the Wildcat – like most other US forces – was held back for the early months of the Pacific War as America embarked on a period of building its capabilities. As action intensified in April and May of 1942, neither the US Navy nor Army Air Forces had yet found a better fighter plane than the Wildcat. Capable or not, it was the best type available for the job.

Aided by a more comprehensive knowledge of the Zero and other Japanese aircraft, American pilots would soon show that any lack of confidence in its abilities

Three US Navy Wildcat F4F-3s – these of a USS *Yorktown* squadron – flying in formation. ✪

were unwarranted and the unlikely hero began to claim a sizeable number of victories – a famous example being the downing of five Japanese bombers over the naval base at Rabaul.

In the battles at Coral Sea and Midway, the Wildcats fought valiantly to force

away intended Japanese invasions of key American territory. In Europe and North Africa, too, British RAF variants were proving their worth in support of major amphibious landings by Allied forces.

By 1943 the American war machine had kicked in, and not only were aircraft leaving factories at an unprecedented rate but significant technological advancements had occurred which finally toppled the Wildcat from its position as the country's premier fighter type.

Even after production ended and the likes of the Hellcat and Corsair overtook it, the Wildcat's work was not done. In the end the type became the only American-built aircraft to serve throughout the Second World War, finding a home on the smaller escort carriers that were unsuitable for the newer and heavier fighters.

As had been the case for nearly every facet of American life at the start of the conflict, the Wildcat was untested in the theatre of war. Despite obvious deficiencies and disadvantages however, when the time came it was not found wanting.

F4F-4 Wildcat fighters, most likely of the US Marine Corps, at Guadalcanal's Henderson field in 1942. ✪

shipping it was set upon. There was nothing pretty about it – the Dauntless was simply instructed to keep slugging away at its weakening enemy until it finally relented. Nor was the SBD committed to any kind of final decisive strike, as had been the Japanese obsession prior to Midway. Like so much of what America produced during the longer conflict, the dive bomber was a weapon of attrition and not one of mass destruction – impressive as the destruction it caused could be. In the final analysis, the SBD's battle report boasted the sinking of six Japanese carriers, 14 enemy cruisers, six destroyers, 15 transports or cargo ships and scores of smaller support vessels. Certainly not a bad return for an aircraft that had been assigned to the scrapheap before fighting had commenced.

Damaged but still standing, an SBD-3 of USS *Enterprise* lands on *Yorktown* after attacking Japanese carrier *Kaga* at Midway. The pilot had to switch ships due to a lack of fuel. ✪

Mitsubishi A6M Zero

"The Zero excited me as nothing else had ever done. Even on the ground it had the cleanest lines I had ever seen in an aeroplane. It was a dream to fly."

Japanese ace Saburo Sakai

This prize naval fighter stands among the most vaunted aircraft of the Second World War, winning plaudits across the globe from allies and enemies alike for its combination of speed, manoeuvrability and range. In Japan it was called Zero-sen (based on the Japanese calendar), the official Allied codename for it was Zeke, but in the west it was known simply as the Zero. Such was its prowess that it survived the entire duration of the conflict.

Its origin can be traced back to 1937 when the Imperial Japanese Navy's premier fighter was the Mitsubishi A5M – a streamlined fuselage with low, forward-set monoplane wings and single seat in the cockpit. This type, however, was old-fashioned; it had an open cockpit from which visibility was poor and its weaponry was just two 7.7mm machine guns.

With its gaze set on expanding into Asia and across the Pacific, the Imperial Navy knew it needed something far more advanced and directed both Mitsubishi and Nakajima to build a model with greater range, enhanced striking power and folding wings. Particular specifications were also requested including a maximum speed of 310mph and the ability to climb to nearly 10,000ft in just three and a half minutes.

Believing the demands to be unachievable, Nakajima did not submit a final design paving the way for its rival Mitsubishi to tick all the boxes required – and the first Zero came into being. The monoplane fighter had a fully enclosed cockpit, fully retractable landing gear, folding wings and visibility was improved by a change to the fuselage design. It was also significantly lighter than any

of its contemporaries, mainly achieved by removing armour from the cockpit, engine and fuel tanks – and there were no self-sealing tanks either. It made pilots and crew extremely vulnerable, but it also made it highly agile. Armament was also upgraded with a combination of two 20mm cannon in the wings and two 7.7mm guns near the engine. Nakajima did retain some involvement, providing the radial piston engine driving a three-blade propeller – although a Mitsubishi powerplant and two-blade propeller was used initially. The Zero also contained a number of technologically superior elements, such as the use of a top-secret aluminium alloy that was being developed by Sumitomo Metal Industries.

The first two A6M1 Type 0 prototypes flew on April 1, 1939, and immediately passed initial testing before being sent for more rigorous naval investigation. During those inspections, the A6M2 Type 0 Model 11 saw the original Mitsubishi engine replaced with the Nakajima – a move that dramatically improved performance. The new version showed such promise that the Navy had 15 built and shipped to China before full testing had finished, and the results were astonishing. It was reported that during one encounter 13 Zeroes shot down 27 enemies in less than three minutes without any losses. The Navy responded by ordering the A6M2 into full production.

Sixty-five of these models had been built when the Model 21 came into production with the introduction of folding wingtips and the improved range courtesy of a 140-gallon wing tank and 85-gallon drop tank. By the time of the Pearl Harbor attack, the Japanese Navy's inventory contained

400-plus Zero fighters and it used them to brutal effect in the early stages of the Pacific conflict.

In 1941, Nakajima introduced its Sakae 21 engine that provided better altitude performance thanks to its two-speed supercharger, and increased engine output to 1130 horsepower. But, the new powerplant was slightly heavier and slightly longer, which meant updates to the Zero were required – the A6M3 Type 0 Model 32 being the result. Design changes to incorporate the enlarged engine meant that top speed was increased by 6mph, but range was reduced by 600 miles. Despite the obvious backward step, the Japanese Navy put the fresh model into production.

The Zero's dominance in aerial dogfights had been what made it so feared, but in reality it was the long-range capabilities it possessed that made it so effective. It was now entirely unsuited to its role of defending Japanese positions throughout the vast Asian and Pacific region it held, and to correct matters the new A6M3 Type 0 Model 22 was introduced. A redesigned wing allowed for a significant increase in fuel tank capacity and the Zero regained its ability to fly on long-range operations. The damage, however, had been done – and having been largely absent from Japan's operations in Guadalcanal and other South Pacific territories the Zero returned to find its country lagging further and further behind in the theatre.

A variety of models were either produced or conceived from variants of the A6M4 through to the final A6M8. By the time of the last Zero model there were fewer than 100 aircraft being produced per month.

KEY FACTS: Mitsubishi A6M2 Type 0 Model 21 Zero

MANUFACTURER:	Mitsubishi (also Nakajima)
PRODUCTION TOTAL (ALL MODELS):	10,815
PRODUCTION DATE:	April 1939
CREW:	1
GROSS WEIGHT:	2410kg
HEIGHT:	10ft, $^{1}/_{16}$in
LENGTH:	29ft, 8 $^{11}/_{16}$in
SPAN:	39ft, 4 $^{7}/_{16}$in
FORWARD WEAPON:	2 x 7.7mm Type 97 machines guns
REAR WEAPON:	2 x wing-mounted 20mm Type 99 cannon
BOMB LOAD:	2 x external 132lb bombs
ENGINE:	Nakajima NK1C Sakae 12, 14-cylinder, air-cooled radial engine
RATED POWER:	950hp
TOP SPEED:	331.5mph
CELLING:	32,810ft
RANGE:	1930 miles

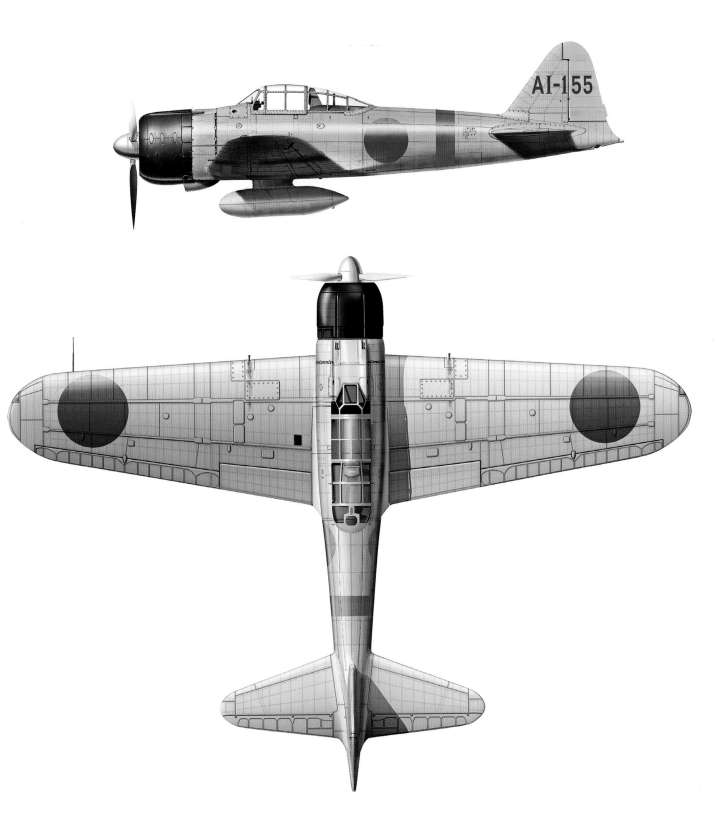

Mitsubishi A6M2 Type 0 Model 21 Zero

The Zero fighter of Lieutenant Commander Shigeru Itaya,
leader of a Japanese fighter squadron. This particular
pilot and aircraft were assigned to carrier *Akagi*, and
were involved in the action at the Battle of Midway
where the mighty vessel was sunk and the Japanese
decisively defeated.

ARTWORK: John Fox

Grumman F4F Wildcat

"I would still assess the Wildcat as the outstanding naval fighter of the early years of World War II. I can vouch as a matter of personal experience, this Grumman fighter was one of the finest shipboard aeroplanes ever created."

British test pilot Eric 'Winkle' Brown

In the Zero, Japan had the brash and confident newcomer. In the early stages of the Pacific War, America's only answer was the wily and durable Wildcat – and it became the unsung hero of the conflict.

Manufacturer Grumman had first begun development of a US Navy fighter in 1935, entering into a competition with rival production firm Brewster. The latter presented its impressive F2A Buffalo – a quick, no fuss single-seater, while Grumman showcased its old-fashioned G-16 biplane design that was presented as the XF4F-1. Brewster's example impressed, while the Navy observers dismissed the Grumman, and it was the Buffalo that went into production.

Undeterred by the setback, Grumman introduced the G-16 model, designated as XF4F-2, and with its more modern monoplane design and a more powerful engine it won admirers – but not enough to dislodge Brewster's F2A as the aircraft of choice. A second revision, however, brought more success.

The G-36 design included a larger wing, a redesigned empennage and the Pratt & Whitney XR-1830-76 engine with a two-stage supercharger. Grumman had got things right, and the American Navy

ordered it into production as the F4F-3.

Performance might have curried favour, but the aesthetics left a little to be desired with a stout fuselage, squared off wings and a basic two-piece cockpit windscreen and slideable canopy.

The Wildcat was never about looking good, though – the only concern was what it could do in the air. Armament came in the form of four .50 calibre machine guns – two on each wing with 450 rounds each – while it was just as quick (331mph) as the Zero and had a better ceiling (39,500 feet). The Zero could travel further, but then America wasn't defending the kind of territory Japan possessed and had little need for long-range fighter at the time.

Entering US Navy service in 1940, an initial batch of 78 examples was ordered – but the Wildcat soon established itself as the premier fighter and quickly demonstrated its superiority to Brewster's F2A Buffalo.

The onset of war meant the two-stage supercharger became a limited commodity, and so a revision was required in the form of the F4F-3A. The new model featured a Pratt & Whitney R-1830-90 radial piston engine with a simpler single-stage, two-speed supercharger – performance was reduced

by the changes and US Navy airmen openly admitted their preference for the original F4F-3 Wildcat.

Having proved its worth as a dogged and dependable fighter, 1942 saw the introduction of the F4F-4 that would become the most-produced aircraft of its day and would perform heroically aboard the American carriers at Coral Sea and Midway. The new model was fitted with six Browning machine guns rather than the previous four – although ammunition wasn't actually increased – and neither was performance; both top speed and rate of climb falling.

What remained, however, was the sturdiness and with pilots able to fly the aircraft in dangerous combat missions with confidence that it would not be easily taken down they could focus their minds on improving tactics to to extract as much a they could from this relatively limited type.

Towards the end of the year and the start of 1943, Grumman began to scale back production of its Wildcat in favour of the new-and-improved Grumman F6F Hellcat. A photographic reconnaissance F4F-7 type was introduced however, and with cameras instead of guns and fuel storage built into the wings it possessed a 3700-mile range.

KEY FACTS: Grumman F4F-4 Wildcat

MANUFACTURER:	Grumman
PRODUCTION TOTAL (ALL MODELS):	7722
PRODUCTION DATE:	1939 (early model development in 1935)
CREW:	1
EMPTY WEIGHT:	2674kg
GROSS WEIGHT:	3617kg
HEIGHT:	9ft, 2½in
LENGTH:	28ft, 9in
SPAN:	38ft
WEAPON:	6 x 12.7mm, .50 cal machine gun
ENGINE:	Pratt & Whitney R-1830-86 double-row radial engine
RATED POWER:	1200hp
TOP SPEED:	320mph
CELLING:	34,000ft
RANGE:	830 miles

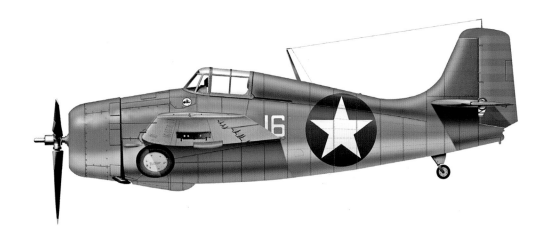

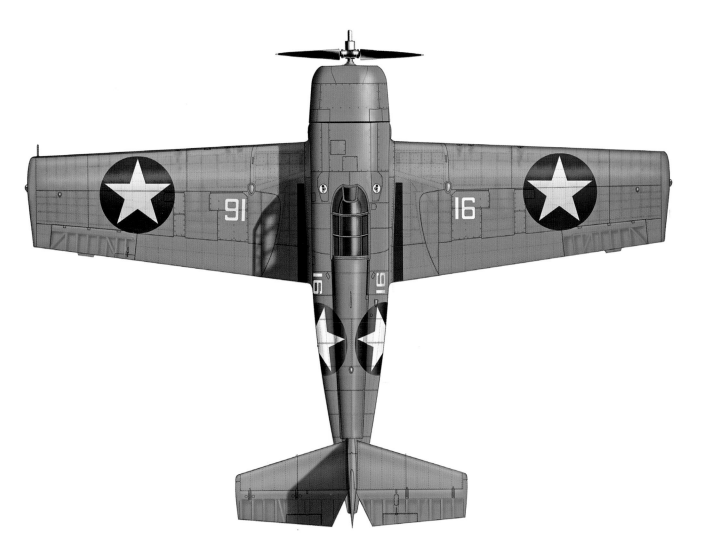

Grumman F4F-4 Wildcat

The Wildcat fighter of Junior Grade Lieutenant Tom Fred
Cheek, section leader of a USS *Yorktown* fighter escort
(VF-3). En route towards the Japanese fleet at Midway,
Cheek's group was escorting a torpedo attack unit when
a large number of Zero fighters separated the party.
Despite the division, Cheek used "skilful tactics and
manoeuvres" to divert the Japanese aggressors from the
US torpedo planes before successfully returning to his carrier.
He was awarded the Navy Cross for his actions.

ARTWORK: John Fox

Douglas SBD Dauntless

"A look-out screamed: 'hell-divers!' The plump silhouettes of the American Dauntless dive bombers quickly grew larger, and then a number of black objects suddenly floated eerily from their wings."

Japanese naval officer Mitsuo Fuchida

This carrier-launched dive bomber was one of America's premier weapons in the Pacific throughout the Second World War, despite the fact that it was a relatively old-timer having first come into production in the mid-to-late 1930s. Even as more advanced warplanes were being churned out of the relentless American factories, the Dauntless soldiered on and defied expectations to strike fear into Japanese sailors. It also proved to be more than a match for the Japanese fighter aircraft charged with defending against it.

Development began as early as 1935 as the Northrop BT-1, but in 1937 the Douglas Aircraft Corporation absorbed Northrop and took over its various projects. The upgraded Northrop BT-2 was completed late the same year, and provided the basis for Douglas to begin full production of the SBD in response to a request from the US Navy for a new dive bomber.

Dauntless design was fairly conventional and a large radial engine was mounted just in front of the cockpit in the extreme forward position of the fuselage. The two-man crew were seated back-to-back, with the pilot in the forward area and a second member manning two .303 machine guns; the pilot acted as the bombardier and was also responsible for two fixed-forward .50 calibre heavy machine guns.

Wings were situated under the fuselage and were noted for their large dive flaps which became synonymous with the series; the perforated 'dive-brakes' – as they became known – were designed to eliminate buffeting during the rapid descent that would occur during bombing runs. The Dauntless was also one of the few carrier aircraft in operation that didn't feature folding wings. Their absence was due to the fact the dive bomber would be subject to the stress of combat dives and climbs, and strong wing support was essential.

Range was impressive at considerably more than 1000 miles, but with a top speed of 250mph and a ceiling of no more than 25,500ft the SBD was vulnerable to attack and required a fighter escort for missions into hostile airspace. Where the type really made its mark, however, was in its payload capabilities. The Dauntless could carry up to 2250lb of ordnance, and its bomb load could be supplemented with depth charges if necessary.

The early model, the SBD-1, had a relatively poor defences with the two .303 machine guns in the fixed-forward position and just one gun covering the rear. Increased fuel capacity was the main update to the SBD-2, but it was the debut of the SBD-3 that showed real signs of what was to come. A bulletproof windscreen was fitted, along with self-sealing fuel tanks and improved armour. The weaponry was also greatly improved, and the four main guns became a series standard. And it was in the third model that the SBD's single Wright R-1820 series air-cooled engine, producing 1000 horsepower, was first installed – the powerplant being utilised throughout the remainder of its production lifespan.

An improved electrical system was the primary change to the SBD-4 model, but then came the SBD-5 – the Dauntless's most-produced incarnation. This new version was given a more powerful R-1820-60 engine that produced 1200 horsepower, and it enjoyed an increased supply of ammunition on board.

Some 2500 of the SBD-5 were built before the development of the SBD-6. The upgrade featured a series of small improvements, including a further jump in horsepower to 1350, but production ended in the summer of 1944.

As well as the standard SBD models, the Dauntless – owing to its range – was also used as a photographic reconnaissance aircraft and was designated accordingly: SBD-1P, SBD-2P, SBD-3P and SBD-4P. The SBD-3, -4 and -5 also spawned a US Army Air Forces equivalent called the Banshee – but this never found the same operational success as its Navy counterpart.

KEY FACTS: Douglas SBD-3 Dauntless

MANUFACTURER:	Douglas Aircraft Corporation, USA
PRODUCTION TOTAL (ALL MODELS):	5936
PRODUCTION TOTAL (SBD-3):	752
PRODUCTION DATE:	March 1941
CREW:	2
EMPTY WEIGHT:	2878kg
GROSS WEIGHT:	4717kg
BOMB LOAD:	1200lb
BOMB SIGHT:	Three-power telescope
PILOT WEAPON:	2 x .50 cal machine gun
REAR WEAPON:	2 x .303 cal machine gun
ENGINE:	Wright R 1820-52
RATED POWER:	1000hp
TOP SPEED:	250mph
CRUISING SPEED:	152mph
CELLING:	25,500ft
BOMBING RADIUS:	250 miles with a 1000lb bomb
SCOUTING RADIUS:	325 miles with a 500lb bomb

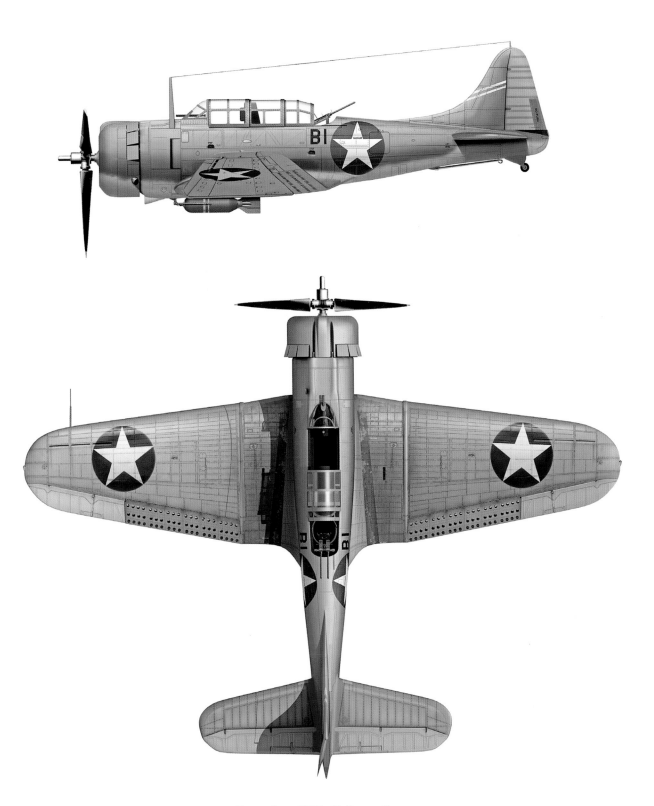

Douglas SBD-3 Dauntless

The Dauntless dive bomber of Lieutenant Commander
Richard Halsey Best, squadron commander of USS *Enterprise*
Bombing Squadron SIX (VB-6). As the aerial attack group
reached the Japanese fleet at Midway, a tactical error
meant that multiple units descended on carrier *Kaga*
rather than spitting between her and flagship *Akagi*.
Best realised the mistake mid-dive, pulled up and then
relaunched. Two more of his squadron joined, and both
released their bombs – the first missing entirely and the
second landing in the water near the stern. The final bomb,
dropped by Best, punched through *Akagi's* flight deck and
exploded in the upper hangar among 18 Japanese B5N2
aircraft. It was this blow that proved to be the fatal hit.

ARTWORK: John Fox

CHAPTER 13

Submarine warfare

Defeat at Midway and a series of setbacks in the South Pacific left Japan on the brink, and the Allied forces pushed home the advantage...

As 1943 arrived momentum had completely shifted in the Pacific Theatre. Having been unable to inflict an early American defeat, despite attempts at Pearl Harbor, Coral Sea, Midway and New Guinea, Japan was now fighting the kind of resource-sapping war it had originally tried so hard to avoid.

America, meanwhile, was buoyant, and the full force of its vast war machine was being felt with an unending supply of aircraft, ships, tanks, weapons, ammunition and other equipment rolling off production lines ready and waiting to be transported to the front lines.

Even when tragedy did strike, America was able to continually bolster its troop numbers with well-rested and well-trained servicemen; Japan's military on the other hand was threadbare.

It meant that the Empire moved to a largely defensive stance while the US, with no need to stake its authoritative position on risky advances, decided to consolidate its positions in the South Pacific territories. The two strategical directions led to a relatively quiet period of the Pacific War, and while there were continued campaigns by US Marines to make land gains, there was no major naval battle for more than two years after the critical period comprising the engagements at Coral Sea and Midway. Despite the lack of any large-scale confrontations, however, the seas were far from tranquil.

The various operations occurring in the island territories were a bloody yet simple case of winning victory by attrition. In reality, the only major tactical decisions for the US to make were which bases to force Japan out of, and which it was able to bypass without having to expend resources or risk personnel. Ocean-based endeavours were far more complex. With both sides – Japan especially – relying heavily on access to shipping routes and their respective abilities to import necessary resources, there was a desperate struggle to gain and maintain control of relevant strategic locations, or impede the respective enemy's abilities to do so.

By this time, both nations possessed sizeable submarine fleets. But while American commanders and strategists had the foresight to direct the vessels at their disposal to target Japanese merchant ships and cripple the country's industry, Japan inexplicably refrained from doing the same and set its submarines to the task of American warship-hunting.

Defeat at Midway and the loss of four carriers might have already sealed its fate, but the strangulation of industrial shipping by Allied submarines made absolutely sure there was no chance of a Japanese revival.

Japanese submarine capabilities

Japan that had spent far more time and resource developing its submarine capabilities than the US, and when conflict began that effort was demonstrated by its advanced and varied fleet of underwater vessels. Its inventory included purpose-built supply vehicles, fleet submarines capable of carrying aircraft, examples capable of the highest submerged speeds of the conflict, and the mammoth *Sentoku* I-400 class – the largest submersible vehicle of the Second World War.

The potential of Japanese submarines as a deadly weapon was also in evidence early in the Pacific Theatre, in fact there is a theory that suggests they were responsible for the sinking of at least one American battleship during the conflict's opening salvoes at Pearl Harbor. Five Japanese midget submarines were present in the waters around Oahu on December 7, and it's believed that at least one made it into the harbour around Ford Island.

These remarkable mini-vessels were as technologically advanced as anything any other nation could boast; each weighed around 50 tonnes, could be operated by a crew of two and was able to carry a fearsome pair of 1000lb torpedoes. They were nimble and fast – with a top speed of 19 knots they would have been able to outrun several of the standard naval types of the day. To reach their target they were fastened to a larger fleet submarine, and then detached – as the quintet was around 12 miles from the mouth of Pearl Harbor late on December 6. It is debatable whether any of these five did strike a blow the following day, but their presence is undeniable – an incredible feat by itself when considering that they had survived the perilous journey across the ocean attached to the back of a 'mother ship'.

What's also undisputed is the success that Japanese submarine operations had against Allied warships. The first major example was another daring raid on an enemy harbour; this time three midget subs entered waters around the port of Sydney in Australia and sank a depot ship – although shots only narrowly missed intended target USS *Chicago*, a heavy cruiser. Other noteworthy kills were the final fatal blows to USS *Yorktown* and USS *Hammann* at the Battle of Midway, plus the sinking of carrier USS *Wasp* in September 1942, anti-aircraft cruiser USS *Juneau* in that same November, escort carrier USS *Liscome Bay* in November 1943, submarine USS *Corvina*

This American government illustration of a Japanese midget submarine was created based on the study of a vessel that was grounded on a Hawaiian beach the day after the Pearl Harbor raid. ✪

A Japanese I-400 class vessel, the largest non-nuclear submarine ever built. ✪

The submarine USS *Nautilus* captures the sinking of Japanese destroyer *Yamakaze* through her periscope in June 1942. ✪

Of the three midget submarines of the Japanese Imperial Navy that entered Sydney Harbour, only one fired on Allied ships. The other pair were both discovered and sunk before they could launch, and this example was pulled from water the following day ✪

the same month and heavy cruiser USS *Indianapolis* in July 1945 – just two weeks before the official surrender.

One of the Japanese vessels capable of carrying aircraft was also responsible for the only aerial bombing attack ever conducted against the continental United States when it launched a Yokosuka E14Y scouting plane that dropped four 168lb bombs in Oregon. The raid, in September 1942, was intended to start forest fires. Earlier that year, a Japanese sub had fired a number of shells at the Elwood Oil Fields near Santa Barbara in California. While neither of these campaigns caused serious damage, they did succeed in striking fear into the population of America's west coast that invasion was a possibility.

Unrestricted American attacks

A critical lack of fuel oil and a loss of air superiority in the Pacific Theatre were two major setbacks that hampered the possibility of further Japanese submarine offensives. But perhaps the most significant reason why Japan failed to fully utilise its impressive fleet was down to the flawed tactics behind their operation.

Japanese high command was insistent that naval battles would be won according to the doctrine of fleet warfare – battleship versus battleship in a grand match-up – but America was not playing by those rules.

Within hours of the Pearl Harbor attack President Roosevelt had ordered unrestricted submarine warfare against Japan. It was a directive that meant sinking any warship, merchant vessel or passenger vehicle in Axis-controlled waters without warning and without aiding survivors.

Submarines accounted for just two percent of the US Navy's total force at the start of the conflict, and many of the types being put to sea were considered obsolete. There were also significant technical problems with their primary weapon – the Mark 14 torpedo – which was considered highly unreliable.

But by the end of 1942, after significant investment in both the submarines and their crews, US vessels were operating out of bases across the Pacific region and along with some British and Dutch examples were strangling Japan with the consistent sinking of both commercial and military vessels.

Towards the end of the Pacific War the destruction of shipping declined, but only really owing to the fact that so few Japanese merchantmen dared to venture out into the open ocean.

Allied submarines sank a staggering 1200 merchant ships throughout the course of the Second World War, and while many of these were smaller cargo carriers, the total included 124 large tankers which were bringing much-needed supplies from the oil-rich Dutch East Indies to the Japanese home islands.

A further 320 transport types were fatally attacked, resulting in the deaths of thousands of Japanese troops en route to crucial campaigns such as the bid to retake Henderson field on Guadalcanal.

Vital oil supplies were being prevented from reaching the mainland, and military personnel and equipment were sunk before they could bolster various island territories – it was a disastrous combination for the Imperial forces.

Submarine warfare went largely unreported to the public at the time – the Allies not wanting to inform the enemy of their intentions or their capabilities – but with the benefit of hindsight the outcome was clear. The Allied submarine offensive was perhaps the single biggest factor in the eventual collapse of the Japanese economy as it veered towards the sobering choice between surrender or continued resistance and potential annihilation.

CHAPTER 14

Allied offensives

The first wave of Marines take cover behind a sand dune on Saipan. The unit is awaiting the arrival of a further three landings. ○

The Allies were in the ascendancy by 1944, and the time had come for America to launch its long-planned island-hopping campaign and put its most powerful new aerial force in range of the Japanese home islands...

The death of Yamamoto, the costly failure of attempts to retake Guadalcanal and the relentless punishment inflicted on Japanese merchant shipping had all taken their toll. Despite the wartime propaganda, morale had begun to ebb away among Japanese citizens, and high command was quickly running out of options to counter the seemingly unstoppable American march through its various overseas territories.

And compounding the catastrophic military losses was the growing divide between the US and Japan in terms of industry; during 1943 American factories were producing 7000 aircraft per month compared to just 1500 in Japan, 500 American destroyers and destroyer escorts had been launched since 1941 compared to just 30 for Japan, and even though the Imperial Navy still held the advantage in terms of carrier production it lacked both the aircraft and trained crew to make the ships a viable offensive of defensive force.

By the middle of the year Allied forces were advancing up through the Solomon Island chain and New Guinea in the same emphatic way in which Japan had moved south at the start of the conflict. Such was the dominance of its South Pacific operations, in November the US and its

partners began a drive to retake land in the central ocean regions, too, and a string of small but strategically significant atolls in the Gilbert and Marshall Islands came under Allied jurisdiction.

In the early weeks of 1944 the US was closing in on the Caroline Islands, but it had never planned an invasion to occupy the naval base at Truk – it was envisaged that too great a force of troops would be needed to manage the vast facility. Instead, with several operating bases now well within reach and a carrier group able to close in, America bombarded the Japanese stronghold from the air to put it completely out of commission.

Japanese commanders on the ground were acutely aware that they were fighting a losing cause, but military-political leaders in Tokyo pressed ahead regardless and continued sending what remained of their personnel and supply reserves to the front lines. A powerful desire to seize the initiative resulted in the decision to simultaneously launch both the long-planned invasion of India and a series of counteroffensives against resisting Chinese troops. Both moves failed spectacularly.

In just four weeks of uncoordinated advances and desperate fighting, British forces repelled the attempted invasion and

Chinese guerrilla tactics blunted Japanese aggression. Even when the Imperial Army units had enjoyed some success, Japan's crippled supply infrastructure meant the advantage was soon lost and soldiers were left in vulnerable positions and under-nourished at best. At worst they were starving to death. As the Japanese slowly retreated, British General William Slim followed and either killed or captured two-thirds of the Japanese force – a total of 50,000 dying as a result of enemy action or through hunger and disease.

With the benefit of hindsight it is clear that there was no way back for Japan at this point. After Midway the country had suffered setback after setback, defeat after defeat – and had been stripped of the resources necessary to turn the tables on the Allies. At the time, however, the Japanese still held vast territories and its major cities remained out of reach for land-based American aircraft.

It meant Japan concentrated its efforts on holding the territories much closer to its home islands. If these could be successfully defended, the American advance might be blunted. Unfortunately for the Japanese, by mid-1944 the American forces thrusting south and those approaching from the centre were ready to meet.

Saipan and the Philippine Sea

On June 15, 1944, an 8000-strong American invasion group disembarked from more than 300 amphibious landing vehicles on the west coast of Saipan – the largest of the North Marianas Islands. It was a move that bypassed territories further south, but American planners knew that they didn't have to take every single land mass and focused on capturing those that were most strategically beneficial.

Saipan became an obvious target after the US had brought the new Boeing B-29 Superfortress long-range bomber into service. It had an operational radius of 1500 miles and if America could establish a base for B-29 units on Saipan then for the first time the Japanese home islands would be well within reach.

The bombardment had begun two days earlier as 15 battleships launched an unrelenting rain of fire against Japanese land positions. The stubborn defenders dug in as US troops began coming ashore, and used heavy artillery, barbed wire and machine gun positions to try and maximize American casualties. By nightfall, however, the Marine divisions had established a six-mile-wide beachhead. Japanese troops counterattacked at night, but suffered significant casualties as they were pushed back. On June 16, infantry divisions advanced on As Lito airfield; once again Japan attempted to counter and once again was defeated. On June 18, the airfield was abandoned, and America finally had control of a runway capable of launching land-based bombers into the heart of enemy territory.

Overwhelmed by the speed and ferocity of the attack, Japanese thinking became more and more muddled. Admiral Mineichi Koga had succeeded Yamamoto as commander-in-chief of the Combined Fleet and had continued his predecessor's ardent belief that the US Navy should be engaged in a single decisive battle. It was a strategy that had cost Yamamoto dearly as he tried and failed to lure the Pacific Fleet out into a 'ship firing upon ship' engagement, but it could be argued Japan's situation was so perilous that only a miraculous naval victory could now change the course of the war.

Whether foolish or the only possible last stand, Koga committed to a grand battle with the Pacific Fleet in early 1944 but the ever growing US naval battlegroup stayed

Japanese aircraft carrier *Zuikaku*, in the centre, and two Japanese destroyers attempt to manoeuvre away from attacks by US Navy aircraft during the Battle of the Philippine Sea. ✪

behind America's advancing front line. As US Navy forces arrived in increasing numbers in the waters around Saipan to support the invasion, senior Japanese Navy admiral Soemu Toyoda decided that this was the time to strike and gave the order. On June 19 the operation began, and what became known as the Battle of the Philippine Sea ensued.

Japan mustered 90% of its fighting fleet – nine carriers, 473 aircraft, five battleships, 28 destroyers and a number of cruisers. It was certainly a sizeable group, but it paled in comparison to the US Fifth Fleet – the new Central Pacific unit – with its 15 fleet carriers, 956 aircraft, seven battleships, 28 submarines, 69 destroyers and a superior group of light and heavy cruisers.

Vice Admiral Jisaburo Ozawa took command at sea, but his pilots were outnumbered and their aircraft were outdated. The only advantage he had was range – having been largely stripped of armour, the Japanese types all had a greater radius and Ozawa used this to position his ships out of reach of American attack groups. He also planned to utilise 500 land-based planes at Guam.

The task forces converged, their numbers ensuring that this engagement would be the largest sea battle of the conflict up to this point – and Ozawa's aircraft roared into the air to get it under way. The attack, however, lacked coordination; the experienced and efficient pilots and crews of the Pearl Harbor raid and other early Japanese offensives had long since departed. Repeated US raids on the land-based portion of Japan's attack neutralised that threat and, due to a US directive to install communications centres on all carriers, Admiral Raymond Spruance was able to anticipate the arrival of the Japanese carrier air groups and launch intercepting Hellcat fighters. US fighter pilots dubbed the subsequent action the Great Marianas Turkey Shoot owing to the ease with which they picked off the advancing Japanese formations, and the few attackers that did reach the US fleet were

met with heavy anti-aircraft fire.

With just one American warship suffering slight damage, attention now turned to launching an aerial counterattack, although the US submarines had already inflicted serious casualties on the first day of the battle having located the Japanese fleet to sink two carriers – Pearl Harbor veteran *Shokaku* and flagship *Taiho*. The loss of these two vessels took the lives of nearly 3000 Japanese crew.

Throughout the night of June 19, American scout planes had searched in vain for the location of the enemy, and the frustration continued throughout the morning and early afternoon of the following day. Finally, a little after 3pm, a USS *Enterprise* reconnaissance aircraft spotted the group and despite its distance and the fact sunset was approaching the opportunity to further weaken Japan's aerial capabilities was too good to miss.

The 240 US fighters and bombers that were launched faced little in the way of defence and managed to destroy the carrier *Hiyo*, while *Zuikaku*, *Junyo* and *Chiyoda* escaped with relatively minor damage. While a final blow had not been delivered in terms of destruction of ships, the loss of aircraft proved much more telling. Clearly defeated, Toyoda ordered Ozawa to withdraw and the battle was over.

Back on Saipan, the Marines faced a determined enemy prepared to fight to the death and suffered considerable numbers of killed and wounded soldiers – 3426 and 10,364 respectively. The consequences for Japan were even more severe however. Of the 30,000 troops tasked with Saipan's defence, fewer than 1000 remained alive when the battle officially ended on July 9. Even more astonishing were the civilian casualties. Huge numbers of Japanese on the island committed ritual suicide rather than face capture. It was one of the Americans' first experiences of Japan's 'death before surrender' doctrine that would have a huge influence over strategic direction as the US navigated its way towards victory.

US forces move towards the beaches of Saipan on June 15, 1944. The ship in the foreground is USS *Birmingham*, while USS *Indianapolis* is also seen firing against Japanese positions. ✪

Leyte Gulf and the Philippines

There had been some debate between American commanders about whether the next move after Saipan should be to invade the Philippines, or bypass this former US territory and move further north to Taiwan. Admiral Nimitz advocated the latter, but General MacArthur was adamant that US forces should return to the island he'd been forced to vacate in early 1942 – and it was an argument he won.

In October 1944, Marines and Army soldiers began landings on the Philippines by way of Leyte Island, and among them was MacArthur himself. Having made the vow "I shall return" he delivered his famous "I have returned" address – the symbolic moment summing up the complete reversal of fortunes that had occurred.

Most American strategists had expected Japan to defend its positions on the Filipino island of Luzon where Japanese air bases in China, Taiwan, Okinawa and Indochina could assist. Instead, off-shore of Leyte, the depleted Japanese Navy gathered its strength for one last effort to cripple the American fleet and the invading force.

A decoy fleet was sent north to lure America's mighty Task Force 34 from the waters around Leyte, and it worked. Japan's remaining group now outnumbered the US units left to defend the invasion, but clever tactical thinking saw the remaining American ships launch sustained raids against the attackers which was enough to pressure the Japanese into withdrawing. Had its ships continued they might have been able to target the vulnerable American invasion party.

As it was, the decision allowed the US to regroup and what followed at the Battle of Leyte Gulf surpassed the Saipan engagement as the largest naval conflict of the Second World War, and by some criteria it remains the largest naval clash in history. With the full concentration of its powerful forces in place, America inflicted a comprehensive and costly defeat on the Japanese – so damaging that it effectively ended the Imperial Navy's ability to continue in the Theatre.

Over the course of four separate smaller skirmishes, Japan lost *Zuikaku* – the last remaining Pearl Harbor carrier – three light carriers, three battleships including the powerful *Musashi*, six heavy cruisers, four light cruisers and nine destroyers. What proved even more damaging, and was the key reason the Japanese Navy was unable to operate after this time, was the distance ships would need to cover for repairs and refuelling. The closest oil supplies were in Singapore, but there were no facilities there for the necessary maintenance.

Repairs could be made in Japan, but oil supplies on the home islands had virtually run dry. Several survivors of the battle did choose a return to the mainland, but many of them would later be bombed and sunk in harbours during American air raids, unable to escape due to lack of fuel.

America would recapture the Philippines, but the campaign was not easy and nor did it come without a price. Here, soldiers take cover behind a trio of advancing Sherman tanks as they move on Imperial Army positions on Panay Island. ✿

With air and sea superiority secured, US troops were able to press home the invasion of Leyte – although as with previous land operations they would encounter stiff resistance from Japanese defenders and would incur significant losses in pursuit of territorial gains.

History suggests that Midway was the point at which the tables turned in the Pacific, but it was America's dominant naval victory and successful invasion of Leyte that signalled the beginning of the end.

It was also the last instance where battleships would fire on each other during a military engagement at sea, and it was the first time Japan utilised a new deadly kamikaze tactic.

The crew of *Zuikaku* salute as the flag is lowered on the listing carrier following an American air strike in the Leyte Gulf. She would later sink and cease to be the flagship of the Imperial Japanese Navy. ✿

General Douglas MacArthur wades ashore during initial landings on Leyte Island in the Philippines ✪

A photograph captured the explosion on America escort carrier USS *St Lo* after she was hit by a kamikaze aircraft on October 25, 1944. ✪

CHAPTER 15

Resistance and surrender

The final chapter of the Pacific War consisted of stubborn Japanese resistance in the face of ferocious American attacks. It would take the debut of a brand-new and history-altering weapon to finally bring about a surrender...

During November 1944, sensing that 1945 could be the final year of conflict, America looked to consolidate its already strong position and began launching B-29 Superfortress raids on Tokyo.

On January 9 the largest force that the US would commit to a single operation – more than 175,000 troops – began landing on the island of Luzon at the heart of the Philippines which was defended by nearly 300,000 Japanese. In total, 10 US divisions and five Filipino regiments battled on Luzon, more troops that the US had used in North Africa, Italy or even southern France.

As had been the case previously, American Army troops were far better equipped and prepared for the battle and quickly made advances – but, also as before, these came at a cost. Japanese tactics were increasingly aimed at ensuring the maximum number of enemy casualties, even without hope of an eventual victory, and after two months of fierce fighting General MacArthur's invasion group had suffered 38,000 soldiers wounded or killed.

The absolute refusal of Japanese troops to back down was costly, both for them and civilians who were armed and incorporated into the defensive formation. Nearly 90% of Japan's defending soldiers were killed in the fighting on the Philippines, and the total number of dead exceeded 400,000 – an indicator of the scale of civilian death.

While the unprecedented destruction continued, America devised campaigns to occupy territory even closer to the Japanese home islands. As hard as it was to believe, the deadliest days of the Pacific War were still to come.

Iwo Jima and Okinawa

Halfway between the Marianas and the home islands, the eight-square-mile island of Iwo Jima became the scene for one of the bloodiest battles of the Pacific Theatre – an encounter that exemplified the horrific war of attrition that was being played out across the region. The Americans intended to capture the small territory and use its three airfields for the aerial bombardment of mainland Japan. The Japanese knew they were unable to hold the territory, but resolved to make the US invaders suffer.

As early as 1944 the island was being transformed into a vast network of traps with the installation of bunkers, fields of barbed wire and machine gun positions. American air raids began in preparation for an eventual invasion as early as mid-1944, but the attacks had little effect on the 11-mile-long network of tunnels that had been dug underground.

On February 19, some 30,000 US Marines came ashore on the south-east coast – precisely the location where much of the Japanese defence had been concentrated. Initially they were unopposed, but as the force pushed inland and hit the first enemy bunker they were met with a hellacious barrage of machine gun and artillery fire. Somehow the Marines managed to push past and reached the west coast by sunset the same day, although the gains had come at the cost of nearly 2000 deaths or injuries.

Just four days later, the Americans would make a key strategical advance to the summit of Mount Suribachi where the now-famous Raising of the Flag on Iwo Jima photograph would be captured – the act becoming a symbol of the hard-fought US victories across the Theatre. It would take another month, March 26, before the entire island was secured and when hostilities ended America was left mourning the deaths of 6800 Marines – with some 20,000 more wounded.

Only 1038 of the 21,000 Japanese defenders were captured alive.

Undoubtedly the most famous image from the Pacific Theatre, as US troops raise the flag atop Mount Suribachi on Iwo Jima. ✪

The battleship USS *Idaho* shells Okinawa on April 1, 1945. ✪

In Burma, China and the South Pacific, Japan was facing continued losses from British, Chinese and Australian campaigns respectively and with the war ending in Europe in May 1945 the combined arsenals of the Allied forces were focused on eliciting Japan's unconditional surrender.

America set its sights on Okinawa, an island just 350 miles from the southern coasts of the main Japanese islands, and on April 1 began landing its latest occupation party. The US intention was to establish airfields for the force of 3000 B-29 bombers it now possessed, as well as to develop a staging area for the planned invasion of Japan that was being tentatively planned for November 1945.

On the ground Okinawa was a bloodbath. Like in Iwo Jima, Japan had dug extensive underground defence systems, and 82 days of brutal battle took place in horrendous conditions. When the US finally won victory there were 12,000 Americans dead or missing, with a further 36,000 wounded. For Japan, 70,000 soldiers of the Imperial Army had been killed, and as many as 150,000 civilians were dead.

The battle for Okinawa also had consequences at sea, as an increasingly desperate Japan launched wave after wave of kamikaze attacks against the supporting US ships. Losses for the American Navy were significant with 12 destroyers and 15 amphibious ships sunk along with 386

vessels damaged, including the carrier USS *Bunker Hill*. While the injuries sustained were greater than anticipated, Japan's defence of Okinawa did bring about the final stand for the Imperial Navy as 10 surface vessels – including *Yamato* – steamed towards the island with the intention of beaching themselves and shelling the American invaders from the coast.

Designated the Ten-Go force, it was spotted by US submarines shortly after leaving Japanese home waters and a group of 300 aircraft attacked it for two devastating hours that eventually sank Japan's prized super battleship. It was an unmitigated disaster, and none of the group ever came close to reaching Okinawa.

US Marines pass the body of a dead Japanese soldier as they advance through Okinawa. ✪

An M4A3R3 'Zippo' Sherman tank, equipped with a flamethrower, attempts to clear a bunker on Iwo Jima. ✪

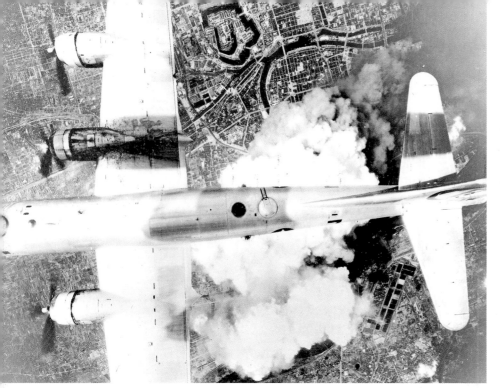

A B-29 Superfortress wreaks devastation on the city below – in this instance, Osaka. ✪

This picture, found in a Japanese school in 2013, shows the mushroom cloud formed by the Hiroshima bomb. It's believed to have been taken about six miles east somewhere between two and three minutes after detonation. ✪

"Prompt and utter destruction"

As the US recovered from deadly battles on Iwo Jima and Okinawa, the appetite for a potential invasion of the Japanese home islands diminished. Instead, the US Navy proposed to force a Japanese surrender through a total naval blockade and sustained aerial bombardment.

With airfields secured much closer to the country's major centres and American desire to use bombing a means of completing victory in the Theatre, operations increased rapidly as the summer of 1945 approached.

One of the most infamous examples was on March 9-10 when an estimated 100,000 Japanese died in fires started by incendiaries dropped from 334 aircraft over Tokyo. Most of the city's buildings were constructed of wood, poorer areas used paper, and the flames completely devastated an area of around 15.8 square miles, leaving more than one million homeless.

Remaining waterway or sea traffic in Japan was limited, but the planned naval blockade also commenced with the mining of rivers and canals from the air, along with the continuation of long-standing unrestricted submarine warfare.

The death of President Roosevelt from

a cerebral haemorrhage on April 12, 1945, led to the inauguration of his deputy Harry S Truman, who continued to advocate the use of firebombing as he weighed the pros and cons of invasion. Would Japan ever realistically surrender? What would be the cost in American lives of a full-scale incursion into the home islands? They were daunting questions, but the top-secret development of a new bomb would save Truman from ever having to answer them.

On July 26, along with the Chinese leader Chiang Kai-shek and British Prime Minister Winston Churchill, Truman issued the Potsdam Declaration that outlined the terms of Japanese surrender and stated that

The burnt remains of Japanese civilians lie on a street in Tokyo after the American fire raids of March 9-10. ✪

if the Empire did not cede to its demands it would face "prompt and utter destruction".

Little did the Japanese know that the US was not referring to further B-29 bombing raids, but instead was warning of the terrible new weapon it was about to deploy. Japan had not heeded the call, and on August 6 was subjected to the world's first ever nuclear attack when America dropped an atomic bomb on the city of Hiroshima. Truman reiterated the terms of surrender, and warned of further devastation "the like of which has never been seen on this earth". Yet again, Japan resisted. But, as promised, three days later a second atomic payload was unleashed on Nagasaki.

The effects of this new super-weapon were on a scale never experienced before. The initial blasts killed thousands, and within the first two days it's believed that anywhere between 150,000 and 200,000 people had succumbed to their injuries or died as a result of the radiation. In the subsequent months, many thousands more died from burns or radiation sickness.

On the same day as the Nagasaki strike the Soviet Union entered Manchuria. Three years on from the crucial turning point of Midway, and Japan was finally beaten.

Surrender

Try as it might, Japan could not regain the initiative after Midway. Its forces were defeated time after time and on each occasion the consequences became more and more severe. The levelling of two entire cities by just two bombs finally broke the Japanese will to resist, and the Pacific War came to an end.

On August 10, the Japanese cabinet accepted the Potsdam terms and on August 15 Emperor Hirohito relayed the news to his fallen nation. Aboard the battleship USS *Missouri* on September 2, a Japanese delegation signed the formal Japanese Instrument of Surrender which was accepted by General MacArthur.

The Allied powers' supreme commander remained in the country to oversee its restoration, while the US assumed a leading role in the development of the postwar world and ascended to its position as a global superpower.

Foreign affairs minister Mamoru Shigemitsu signs the official Japanese surrender on board USS *Missouri* in Tokyo harbour, under the watchful eyes of American General Richard K Sutherland, and other US Navy personnel. ✪